THE CAMPOUT

COOKBOOK

**ALSO AVAILABLE FROM
MARNIE HANEL AND JEN STEVENSON**

The Picnic

Summer: A Cookbook

The Snowy Cabin Cookbook

THE
CAMPOUT
COOKBOOK

Inspired Recipes for Cooking
Around the Fire and Under the Stars

MARNIE HANEL & JEN STEVENSON

Illustrations by Emily Isabella

ARTISAN | NEW YORK

Library of Congress Cataloging-in-Publication Data

Names: Hanel, Marnie, author. | Stevenson, Jen, 1977- author.
Title: The campout cookbook : inspired recipes for cooking
around the fire and under the stars / Marnie Hanel and
Jen Stevenson.
Description: New York, NY : Artisan, a division of
Workman Publishing Co., Inc., 2018. | Includes index.
Identifiers: LCCN 2017040390 | ISBN 9781579657994
(hardcover : alk. paper)
Subjects: LCSH: Outdoor cooking. | LCGFT: Cookbooks.
Classification: LCC TX823 .H29 2018 | DDC 641.5/78—dc23
LC record available at https://lccn.loc.gov/2017040390

Design by Renata Di Biase

Artisan books are available at special discounts when
purchased in bulk for premiums and sales promotions as
well as for fund-raising or educational use. Special editions
or book excerpts also can be created to specification. For
details, contact the Special Sales Director at the address
below, or send an e-mail to specialmarkets@workman.com.

For speaking engagements, contact speakersbureau@workman.com.

Published by Artisan
A division of Workman Publishing Co., Inc.
225 Varick Street
New York, NY 10014-4381
artisanbooks.com

Artisan is a registered trademark of Workman Publishing Co., Inc.

Published simultaneously in Canada by Thomas Allen & Son, Limited

Printed in China

10 9 8 7 6 5

For survivalists
with standards

Contents

Preface

Who hasn't gazed around a campfire and been keenly aware of how happy they are? Rendered rosy by the fire glow (or possibly the flask cocktails), full of a comforting supper, with a night of stargazing, chin-wagging, and s'mores-roasting ahead, one can't help but triumph in the joy of leaving everything behind, aside from food and fellowship. It's a bliss we've chased since childhood.

We arrived at *The Campout Cookbook* from different trails. For Jen, camping connotes memories of family trips during which she'd innocently circle the campground on her Huffy bicycle, scouting the tip-top site and pouncing at the first sign of other campers' imminent departure. Only then would her family set up their rustic residence, a well-considered wonderland complete with a proprietary kitchen, living room, and, most important, camp shower. They'd roast franks over the fire, see national parks through a sizeable tent flap, and swat mosquitoes en masse. For Marnie, camping brings back memories of out-of-her-depth adventures away: summer-camp canoe trips in the Canadian Boundary Waters complete with

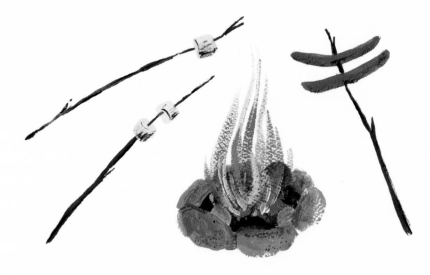

foibles and foil packets, a weeklong kayak trip tracing the path of Peter Puget through the San Juan Islands, and a monthlong rafting trip through the Southwest. She really had to paddle (and portage) for her pancakes.

Our stories converge in Portland, Oregon, where camping is, to our mutual delight, de rigueur but not necessarily rigorous. Portlanders think nothing of bringing into the woods a cutting board piled high with charcuterie, a twelve-component salad for every guest present, and a bounty of grillables. It's a function of both culture and geography; when you live in a food town where the farmers' market and natural wonders are equally accessible, there's no need to sacrifice on either front. Rather, a campout becomes an extended picnic. (And, goodness knows, we love those. So much so that we wrote a book, *The Picnic: Recipes and Inspiration from Basket to Blanket*, on the subject.) Campsites top picnic sites with one thrilling amenity: the fire pit.

Although it's quite literally the oldest trick in the cookbook, fire-cooking feels fresh and exciting.

We've become so accustomed to the precision and reliability of the home kitchen that it's freeing to see how successful you can be when cooking off the (buffalo-checked) cuff. The campfire cooking recipes in this book all include an ideal cooking temperature and instructions on how to approximate that in a fire pit (see page 26 for the master chart), but since accuracy goes out the window when you're not turning a dial, you'll need to rely on your intuition and senses to get where you need to go. When your efforts are successful, the output of your inexact alchemy will feel like pure magic. (We imagine that Cro-Magnon man let out that same gleeful squeal when unveiling his own Double-Decker Pineapple Mug Cakes, page 156.) And when your efforts are less successful, we highly recommend you break off the bottom of those charred biscuits, spread a little jam on the pleasantly flaky tops, and congratulate yourself on not settling for a rehydrated meal. To be clear: You will burn some of the food in this book. That's okay! You're camping. Camp food doesn't need to turn out perfectly to be absolutely perfect. (The fact that you cooked it outside gives you a lot of leeway.) But if you're not willing to leave your perfectionism at the ranger station, you can always eschew the campfire in favor of old faithful, the camp stove.

We hope you'll plan your provisions with an eye to mixing and matching camp-cooking styles, and upping your fire game over time. Since campers vary in their desire to cook actively at the campground, we've written the recipes keeping in mind what can be prepped at home. Several recipes, such as the trail snacks, stews, and braises, can be made entirely in your kitchen ahead of the campout. (As you get more comfortable with fire-cooking, you're welcome to attempt many of these on-site, swapping the stovetop for the campfire and the convection oven for the Dutch oven; just be sure to pack *a lot* of lump charcoal.) Other recipes are designed to be prepared on the fly; if you've caught an impressive trout, or purchased an impressive rib-eye, we'll tell you what to do with it. But most of these recipes split your brave efforts between the home and

camp kitchens, honoring our early camping motto, "Be prepared," and our current one, "Prepare to be impressed." To achieve both, be sure to check the "In the Backpack" packing lists that follow some recipes so you'll have all the equipment you'll need.

Camping and nostalgia form something of a buddy system, so we've tried not to leave any classic (particularly the kitschiest) behind. From bug juice to beans to banana boats, tinfoil dinners and pudgie pies, gorp and the almighty s'more, it's all here, with updates for today's fresh ingredients and way of eating. And we've tried to give you enough variations to keep your campers intrigued for a lifetime of overnights in the backcountry. Because you know what's better than one s'more, foil-packet, or pancake-topper recipe? Twelve. Of each.

This book is designed for car campers, as you might suspect if you've ever tried to hike with a 12-inch cast-iron Dutch oven. If you're an avid backpacker, pursue success and avoid sciatica by sticking to the lightweight recipes (long live jerky and trail mix) and save the plein air pizza night for a backyard shindig with an outdoor fire pit, or even your kitchen table. The recipes work equally well in the great indoors.

Our aim is to make camp cooking clever and fun, with the none-too-subtle intention of convincing everyone to do it more often. Our campouts aspire to be the greatest parties you've ever attended, getaways where the details feel thoughtful but not laborious, where everyone pitches tents and pitches in, and where the memories of what you ate help you hold on to the details of where you went and what hilarity ensued, because we love to laugh as much as we love to cook.

Now let's get camping! And be sure to show off your feasts in the forest as you do. Join us on Instagram at #thecampoutcookbook.

xo,
Marnie and Jen

Chapter 1

From Backpack to Bonfire

Whether you venture into the great outdoors weekly, annually, or centennially, it's imperative to hit the trail with a spirit of adventure, the proper fire-making and -cooking tools, and enough enamelware to host an entire Scout troop. (You never know.) This camping compendium will guide you in selecting the perfect campsite and means of shelter, setting up the consummate camp kitchen, mastering the many quirks of cast-iron cooking, and using your trusty thermos to its full potential. Perhaps most important, never again forget the matches *or* the telescoping marshmallow-roasting sticks, thanks to the handy packing checklist at the end of the chapter.

Camping Compendium

While there's much admiration to be had for those spontaneous souls who can toss a rucksack in the Jeep and hit the hinterlands on a whim, a bit of planning can elevate an otherwise routine camping excursion into a real forest fête. Follow these camp commandments to craft a cozy and comfortable glampout to remember.

Scope a Five-Star Site

If you've ever been assigned a swampside setting, you're well aware that not all campsites are created equal. Hopefully, you've already reserved your favorite slice of lakefront heaven, but if you're bravely heading into the first-come-first-served unknown, score the best site by arriving on the early side (or right around checkout time), consulting the campground rules and regulations board for proper protocol, and scouting the entire loop before committing to a spot—because nothing spoils a good time more than campsite regret.

Bring the Basics

Best not to assume that the campground will stock essentials like soap, toilet tissue, and dry firewood. Taking the "What's in Your Backpack?" list on page 40 and checking it twice can help you sidestep bug-spray-and-cast-iron-skillet-scarcity-related heartache; or, better yet, keep a plastic tub of "can't camp withouts" at the ready should an invitation to hit the open road arrive unexpectedly (see page 131).

Pack Heavy

All your life, you've been schooled in the virtues of packing light, but for a truly cozy and comfortable car camping experience, it's best to err on the side of packing *heavy*. After all, you'll never regret having extra blankets, water, propane, and whiskey, but underestimating your group's D-battery and coffee-bean consumption is a major backcountry bungle, especially if the nearest general store is the next mountain range over.

Pimp Your Pantry

Leaving your impeccably stocked pantry and electricity-fed freezer in the rearview doesn't mean sacrificing creature comforts like spices, ice cream, and caviar. (Okay, fine, maybe the beluga can stay home.) Use dry ice to fortify the camp cooler, invest in a collapsible cupboard or an "Ultimate Camp Kitchen" (page 39) for easy ingredient organization, and build a restaurant-worthy mobile seasonings set using slide-top tins or 4-ounce jelly jars.

Primp Your Partyware

Sure, it's simpler to use compostable plates and cups, or the beloved Technicolor plasticware from childhood camping trips of yore, but that won't do justice to this gorgeous food. Pack a stack of pretty oilcloth or washable tablecloths, procure a set of inexpensive silverware and enamelware place settings, pack the stemless wineglasses and bar kit, and don't skimp on the serveware— you'll use those melamine platters more than you think.

Dish Out Din-Din Duty

Unless you've got the luxury of a designated camp cook, divvy up the dining duties well before departure. Depending on the size of your camping party and the duration of the trip, assign KP by meal or day, with all noncooks picking up table-setting, dishwashing, and fire-stoking responsibilities. To encourage creativity (and perhaps a bit of friendly competition) among a group of campers, start a shared menu online, and get the group buzzing about the fire-kissed feasts to come.

Rally the Booze Brigade

Whether it's a pleasant after-dinner diversion or the only thing that gets you through a weekend in the wilderness, there's no downplaying the importance of a well-mixed drink enjoyed campfireside. If your party includes a skilled and willing bartender, collect a cocktail kitty via Venmo, and put him or her in charge of the camp saloon. Otherwise, implement a BYO (and some to share) policy, and monitor supplies daily to avoid midnight moonshine shortages.

Chill Out:
Packing the Camp Cooler

Serving as your satellite refrigerator, your camp cooler performs a vast number of vital duties—fish froster, guacamole guardian, salad keeper, rosé chiller, and overall food-safety sheriff. We recommend lugging at least two ice chests: one for the food and one for refreshments—because beer and Blood Orange Bug Juice (page 165) need their personal space.

Polar Pre-funk
If your cooler's been sitting in a sweltering summer garage, ready it for camp kitchen action by bringing it indoors a day before the trip and dumping plenty of ice inside a few hours before you pack it.

As Cold as Ice
Don't underestimate the value of pre-cooling—it takes 2½ pounds of ice to chill a gallon of room-temperature liquid. To prolong the brrr, freeze any provisions that are not meant to be consumed at the first meal, such as marinated meat, cheese, butter, bread, cinnamon rolls, milk, juice, and bottled water.

Arctic Layering
Layer securely wrapped raw meats and fish first, followed by frozen dairy, deli meats, bread, eggs, and condiments, then delicate fruits and vegetables. Chocolate for s'mores needs safeguarding from heat, cold, *and* moisture, so place it in a resealable plastic bag and store it on the very top, avoiding direct contact with ice.

Ice, Ice, Baby
Plan on ¾ to 1 pound of ice per quart capacity of your cooler—cubed ice is ideal for short-term cooling, while block ice holds down the frigid fort. Use blocks or large flat reusable ice packs as your foundation, then scatter cubes between each layer of provisions and on top, letting them work their way in between bottles and bundles to provide surround chill. Wrap dry ice in newspaper or old towels and place it on top of items that require a real boreal blast, like ice cream.

Throw Shade
At the campsite, make sure the cooler's sequestered in the shade. If you're pitching a tent in the Mojave, at the very least push the ice chest under the picnic table (never leave it in a hot trunk). Melted ice holds the cold better than air, so don't drain the water until absolutely necessary (to avoid soggy salami or Swiss cheese, put susceptible floaters in gallon-size resealable plastic bags), and keep the lid closed tightly at all times (one more reason to seclude the oft-visited sips stash in its own cooler).

5 Fantastic Car Games

A car ride is all fun and games until an hour or so into the road trip, when the horizon seems endless. Break up the monotony of the open road, glean insight into your traveling companions' souls, and stave off backseat squabbles and turf wars with these five classic crowd-pleasers.

1. 20 Questions

This oldie but goodie operates on a simple premise—one player thinks of a person, place, or thing (e.g., Ranger Smith, Camp Ivanhoe, sleeping bag onesie), and the rest of the group gets twenty yes-or-no questions to guess what it is. Best played with strong deductive reasoners and nonpsychics.

2. Slug Bug (aka Punch Buggy)

For obvious reasons, games that involve legally punching people you're confined with in close quarters are eternally popular, so resurrect this childhood favorite, which permits players to sock their fellow passengers in the bicep whenever they spot a classic Volkswagen Beetle or van. Reasonable regulations apply—show full respect for the "no punch back" clause, never punch the driver, and cease punching in the vicinity of a VW dealership.

3. License Plates for Logophiles

Upon encountering a lettered license plate, all players come up with a word that includes all the letters in order. For an added twist, the words must be camping themed. For example, FLH becomes "flashlight," CTN becomes "canteen," and BRE becomes "bobcat repellent." Or something like that.

4. Would You Rather . . . ?

An excellent opportunity for the creative, quirky, and downright warped to show their stuff, this game's line of questioning can quickly escalate from the relatively benign ("Would you rather eat a whole jar of horseradish mustard or a package of uncooked hot dogs?") to the truly terrifying ("Would you rather share a two-person tent with your mother-in-law or be rolled in gorp and locked in the campground bathroom with a hungry honey badger?").

5. The Quiet Game

However you frame the rules, the name of this game is *shhh*.

Scout Your Spot

It may take several trips around Loops A, B, *and* C, but picking the perfect campsite is serious business. After all, this petite patch of nature is your home for the next few days, so you want to be sure there's running water, fetching flora and fauna, and *plenty* of room for the camp kitchen.

Topography

- ☐ Level, dry, sharp-rock/massive-root-free terra firma (bonus points for tent-friendly grass)
- ☐ Devoid of yellow jacket nests, ant colonies, and snake holes
- ☐ Burbling stream or river within a hardtack's toss
- ☐ Well above dry streambeds or flash-flood plains
- ☐ Panoramic views (preferably a highly photogenic mountain range or ocean)

Amenities

- ☐ Picnic table
- ☐ Water faucet
- ☐ Fire pit
- ☐ Bear locker
- ☐ Ample supply of forageable firewood/camp host who sells firewood

Not Within 100 Feet of the Site

- ☐ Trash bins
- ☐ Bathrooms (particularly of the vault toilet variety)
- ☐ Sizeable patches of poison oak or poison ivy
- ☐ Bodies of stagnant water emitting a gentle buzz
- ☐ Bear tracks/den/cubs

If you've checked all the boxes, you're ready to camp in comfort!

Which Lean-to Are You?

This flowchart will help you choose just the right sleeping scenario based on your interpersonal preferences, availability of natural resources, and whether you remembered the tent.

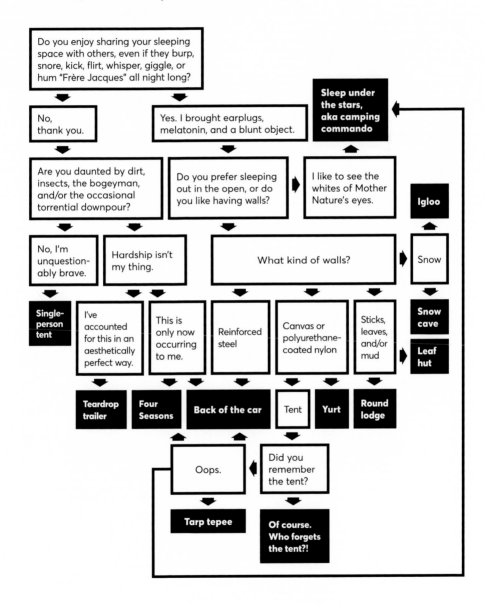

Congratulations! You can now camp like a champ.

Now We're Cooking with Gas

A flickering fire may be the most atmospheric way to sizzle your sausage, but the undisputed king of the camp kitchen is the classic propane (aka white gas) camp stove. Effortless to operate, impervious to Mother Nature's wet and windy whims, and sturdy enough to transcend generations (one of us still owns the same hunter green Coleman from our childhood camping trips), these reliable, weather-resistant workhorses should be the first thing packed after the tent. Here's why.

Butane Backup
Regardless of the weather report's promises, country skies can switch from sunny to surly in the blink of an eye. A powerful double-burner camp stove (or even a space-saving canister stove or inexpensive single-burner butane stove) lets you warm up pre-prepared stews and chili, heat tortillas, and simmer hot cider, even if you have to do so swathed in a waterproof poncho and huddled beneath a breezy camping canopy or high-hung tarp. If it's blustery, most camp stoves have a built-in windshield; in a pinch, improvise with a foil screen.

Canister Count
With light use (boiling water, brewing tea and coffee, scrambling eggs), a propane canister or two can last the entire weekend, but if you're cooking substantial meals using both camp stove burners, plan on a full 1-pound canister per meal, just to be on the safe side.

Up Your No-Flame Game
When installing or removing a fuel cartridge, make sure there are no open flames nearby. Keep canisters upright when transporting them, store them outside, and carefully dispose of them as indicated on the label. And only use cartridges specifically designated for your particular stove.

Go with the Flow
Never, ever operate your camp stove indoors or in a confined space (like a tent or the back of the car), as this can lead to carbon monoxide poisoning or fire. Make sure you set up the stove in a well-ventilated area, and never leave it unattended.

Stop, Drop, and Smother
In the event of a camp stove grease or oil fire, gently smother the flames with a metal lid, or, in dire cases, employ your fire extinguisher. (Because you most definitely brought a fire extinguisher.)

Light My (Camp) Fire

When forging through the frontier, nothing is more important than (wo)man's best camping friend—*fire*—especially when you've got a meal plan that far transcends hardtack and wild-foraged acorns. When the time comes to heat things up, follow these simple steps to build a foolproof fire, then safely smother it.

Buy Local . . . Logs
Some campgrounds outlaw BYO firewood in order to squash the possibility of non-native creepy crawlies hitching a ride, so check the rules and regulations before you leave, and as a general rule of thumb, don't transport wood more than 50 miles from its home.

Burn, Baby, Burn?
Before you start stacking sticks, make sure no burn bans are in place, and that recreational fires are allowed in your campground. If camping off the grid, procure any necessary permits.

Three's Company
The best-laid blazes require the holy trinity of *tinder* (twigs, bark, dry leaves and grass, chocolate bar wrappers, belly button lint), *kindling* (slim sticks roughly the diameter of a hot dog), and *firewood* (preferably dry logs, unless you're trying to send a smoke signal).

The Cone Zone
Pile a bountiful bundle of tinder in the middle of your fire pit, then arrange kindling in a cone around it, tepee-style. Build a second tepee made of firewood around the kindling, then light the tinder and watch the flames leap. When the cone collapses, stack more logs atop your alfresco inferno.

Learn and Burn
If you have, in fact, forgotten the waterproof matches or lighter, please see "Darling, Disaster! 10 Camping Crises Averted" on page 36 for creative fire-starting solutions, including but not limited to flint-and-steel, magnifying glass, and Coke-can-and-chocolate-bar.

No Ember Left Behind
When you've finished your last Off-the-Grid Old-Fashioned (page 160) and are ready to turn in for the night, pour water on the campfire ashes, stir them with something other than your hand, check thoroughly for escaped coals, and continue adding water until you are completely certain that every last spark has been smothered.

No Bonfire, No Breakfast
Rise at the crack of dawn and repeat—Dutch oven cinnamon rolls (page 214) and kielbasa potato hash (page 202) await.

Keep the Spark Alive: Fire Tools

Sometimes it's okay to play with fire, and when you do, it's best to have these nifty tools on hand to help stoke, poke, and roll. Just remember, only you can prevent forest fires, spark-seared camping chairs, pool-float pyres, and tent flambé.

Campfire Claw
If you're fond of your bangs and eyebrows as is, extra-long metal tongs let you manhandle blazing logs without sacrificing your forehead fringe.

Barbecue Tongs
When getting up close and personal with the fire pit grill, a sturdy pair of wood-handled barbecue tongs will keep things from getting *too* hot and heavy.

Oven Mitts
In the line of camp cook duty, it's all too easy to brush up against a near-molten pan handle, so pack a pair of extra-tough oven mitts made of silicone, aramid fibers, or, ideally, dragon scales.

Lid Lifter
Head off cast-iron-Dutch-oven burns at the pass with this simple but invaluable metal fork, meant for lifting the oven lid (e.g., to taste-test the Spicy Chuckwagon Chili, page 108).

Tripod
Take your cast-iron game airborne with a campfire cooking tripod, which lets you dangle beef-stew-filled Dutch ovens and pots of cowboy coffee over the open flame.

Rolla Roaster
These ingenious telescoping marshmallow roasters extend nearly 4 feet, putting plenty of distance between you and the flaming chunk of sugar that will soon be your dessert.

Big Stick
When all else fails, slip into the woods and seek that most timeless of fire tools—the big stick, which is also useful in times of marshmallow-roasting, tent-staking, splint-tying, and wolverine-attack crisis.

Now We're Cooking with Fire

The camp stove (reliable, adjustable, portable) has its merits, but the campfire (fickle, fascinating, dangerous) has our undying love. Cooking on it is pure magic. To succeed in this most primitive kitchen, toss out perfectionism, embrace intuition, follow your nose (it's how you'll know something is burning), and review these instructions.

That's the Pits

It's always the best practice to use an existing pit for fire-cooking, but if you find yourself needing to build your own, make sure to stay 10 yards away from any flammables (e.g., your sleeping bag), dig down to the dirt, and construct a ring of rocks or cinder blocks (if camping near a construction site) or bury a metal ring (wow, you thought ahead!) to contain the flames. If you're camping in your own backyard, we recommend using a purpose-built fire pit (we love our Landmann) rather than risk scorching the sod.

BYOG

Many campgrounds provide a grate on the fire pit, but it's always a good idea to BYOG (Bring Your Own Grate) just in case. Pick up a camping grate with folding legs from an outdoor gear supplier, and a grill grid or two from your favorite kitchen store to avoid packing in a grill brush to clean the provided grate or watching your vegetables slip through its (often too wide) slats.

Wood You Rather?

Few things (frankfurters, secret wills) are suited to roasting over an open flame. Rather, prime cooking conditions are achieved on hot coals. Create them the effortful but romantic way by burning a bundle of dry firewood until the coals are mostly white. Using a campfire claw or a big stick (see page 146), move any still-flaming pieces of wood to the side of the pit.

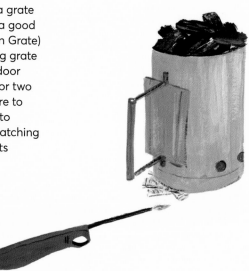

Old King Charcoal

Or, for a swifter setup and/or ready replenishing, snag a bag of charcoal. We prefer hardwood lump charcoal for camp-cooking. It's not soaked in chemicals, so it smells like something that *should* touch food; it imparts smoky flavor; and it's rather exciting. Plan on bringing one small bag for every meal you cook on the fire. Hardware stores, Trader Joe's, and most grocery stores carry it. (If you prefer your dad's briquettes, those'll work, too.)

A Real Flame Changer

Plunk down $15 for a charcoal chimney starter (or two!) and never again suffer charcoal-lighting woes. Fill the chimney with charcoal, set it on the campfire grate, stuff newspaper under the base, light the paper, and wait 15 minutes until all the charcoal turns grayish white. Then dump your not-so-hard-earned coals into the fire pit. If you're preparing a meal with a prolonged cooking time (e.g., lasagna or pizzas), start a new batch of coals right away.

On the One Hand

Using a fire tool, grade the coals so that they're deeper and very hot in half the cooking area and sparse and cooler in the other. Position the grate so that it's 6 inches or so above the coals. Now summon your bravery and check the heat by holding your hand 5 inches above the grate. If you want to pull away in 2 to 4 seconds, you've reached high heat. In 5 to 7 seconds? Medium. In 8 to 10 seconds? Low. In 1 minute? Start the camp stove.

All Fired Up

Charcoal oxygenates quickly in an open fire pit, so you'll need to replenish it every 30 to 45 minutes, as needed. Either use the chimney to start a fresh batch or add a new round of charcoal to the still-hot coals a half hour after you start cooking. Once you pull the food off the fire, throw on a few logs for warmth and ambiance, dish out the grub, and put up your boots.

Go Dutch

To spare you charred-enamel-induced heartache, please note that a camping Dutch oven is a footed cast-iron pot with a rimmed lid, *not* your heirloom Le Creuset. This witchy wilderness workhorse can reheat soup, bake a batch of mug cakes, *and* bear-proof your butter (when hoisted up a tree).

For a 10-inch footed Dutch Oven

Temperature	325°F	350°F	375°F	400°F	425°F	450°F
Coals Over/Under	13/6	14/7	16/7	17/8	18/9	19/10

For a 12-inch footed Dutch Oven

Temperature	325°F	350°F	375°F	400°F	425°F	450°F
Coals Over/Under	13/7	14/8	16/8	17/10	18/10	19/11

You Have Chosen Wisely

If forced to choose among your darlings (every trunk has its limits), select a shallow Dutch oven for anything that wants a browned or crunchy top (e.g., Buttermilk Biscuits, page 208) and pick a deep Dutch oven for slow simmerers (e.g., Backcountry Beef Stew, page 110).

Hot and (Not) Bothered

Cast iron is slow to warm, so preheat your Dutch oven for 10 minutes when dealing with recipes that require a quick burst of direct heat (e.g., a Dutch baby). To keep things cooking evenly, rotate the oven and lid every 15 minutes and replenish the coals every 30 to 45 minutes.

Set the Oven

The number of coals surrounding the Dutch oven determines its cooking temperature. To roughly estimate how many coals you'll need to reach 375°F, double Dutch's diameter and place one-third of that sum underneath and two-thirds on the lid in an evenly-spaced circle. (For example, a 12-inch Dutch oven calls for 8 coals under it and 16 coals on the lid.) Or, if mental math isn't your thing, refer to the more precise chart above from Lodge, the kings of cast iron. This chart is devised for charcoal briquettes, so when cooking with lump charcoal, or firewood coals, think of each unit as a portion roughly that size.

Peek-a-Whew

We wish you a calm and collected fire-cooking experience, but don't be surprised if when you really get going out there, between the rotations and the replenishing, the coal ratio gets tossed out the window and it turns into coal chaos. Remember, you can always slow down by taking the Dutch oven off the heat, and, when in doubt, a lift of the lid will tell you everything you need to know. For better or worse, but usually better. We swear!

Cast-iron Commandments

Cast-iron cookware has survived *thousands* of years, so why does it seem likely to self-destruct now that it's in your hands? Quell the fear factor as follows.

Season's Greetings

Cast iron is protected by its seasoning: layers of oil baked into the pan to create a nonstick surface. Even if it arrives pre-seasoned, offer it some attention. Give it a good scrub, dry it, heat it on the stovetop to *really* dry it, and, once it's cool, rub it with 1 to 2 teaspoons of unsaturated oil, such as canola, vegetable, or flaxseed. Now buff it with a paper towel and place it upside down in a 400°F oven for an hour. After each use, reapply a little oil before storing. Use your cast iron as often as possible—the more love you give it, the more it will return.

Is Soap a Nope?

Cast-iron diehards abhor the sight of suds, which endanger the seasoning unnecessarily. (Germs can't live on this hot a pot, so soap is beside the point.) But, in truth, your skillet will survive a scrubbing, and you'll likely reach for the dish detergent to de-soot. The real threat to the pot's hard-earned coating is moisture, so don't store your Dutch oven in a garden shed or put it away wet. Should that happen, you'll certainly need soap to remove the rusty evidence. Reseason as instructed at left.

Gray Ladies

There once were two cookbook authors who baked a sumptuous berry slump in a brand-spanking-new Dutch oven and ate it with glee, only to discover that it had turned their teeth blackish. After they got over the shock and brushed their teeth twenty-seven times, they vowed never to simmer anything acidic in cast-iron cookware until the seasoning is well established. We suggest you do the same.

Go on, Put Baby in the Corner

Despite what you've heard about cast iron, there's no reason you can't stack it, use metal utensils on it, hike Mount Everest with it, buy lots of it, or construct a fort entirely of it to live in forever. We'll visit you there.

Tips & Tricks: Tools

The following household items will help you enjoy the creatures in comfort.

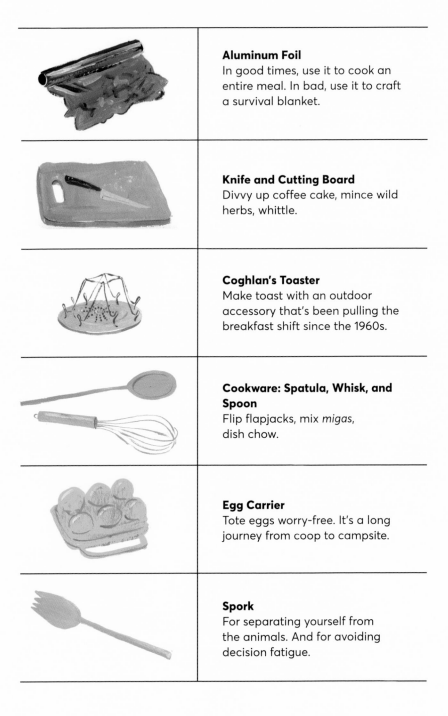

Aluminum Foil
In good times, use it to cook an entire meal. In bad, use it to craft a survival blanket.

Knife and Cutting Board
Divvy up coffee cake, mince wild herbs, whittle.

Coghlan's Toaster
Make toast with an outdoor accessory that's been pulling the breakfast shift since the 1960s.

Cookware: Spatula, Whisk, and Spoon
Flip flapjacks, mix *migas*, dish chow.

Egg Carrier
Tote eggs worry-free. It's a long journey from coop to campsite.

Spork
For separating yourself from the animals. And for avoiding decision fatigue.

Rimmed Baking Sheet	Biscuit-prep station, makeshift griddle, steak holder, hot pad, and magnetic letter board.
Metal Bowl	Mix dough, toss salads, gather wild berries, whip cream, wash your face— what *can't* you do with it?
Mason Jar	Pulls quintuple duty as a measuring cup, drinking glass, vase, lantern, and yellow jacket trap.
Mesh Laundry Bag	Air-dry camp dishes, organize beach toys, wrap around food to keep lusty bugs at bay.
Belt and S-Hooks	Buckle a belt to a tree and use S-hooks to hold pots, pans, utensils, and small disobedient children.
Collapsible Wagon	Unfold upon arrival, assign to schlep duty, then send out on kindling-gathering expeditions.

99 Ways (and Counting) to Use a Thermos

1. Car keys holder
2. Hot cocoa dispenser
3. Hot dog warmer
4. Wildflower vase
5. Drum
6. Mug dryer
7. Wasp trapper
8. Martini shaker
9. Tomato soup holder
10. Hooch hider
11. Time capsule
12. Ice bucket
13. S'mores-stick holder
14. Bogeyman basher
15. Suboptimal rolling pin
16. Coffee cup
17. Kool-Aid cooler
18. Napkin weight
19. Moonshine still
20. Fire douser
21. Rainstick
22. Specimen collector
23. Valuables safe
24. Flashlight rest
25. Tent site tamper
26. Tent stake hammer
27. Truffle basket
28. Whipped cream whipper
29. Chipmunk feeder
30. Cafeteria collateral
31. First-aid kit
32. Urn
33. Meat tenderizer
34. Imprudent flyswatter
35. Ice chipper
36. Smashed-potato smasher
37. Daisy planter
38. Kibble container
39. Drill bit case
40. Rock tumbler
41. Porridge pot
42. Cup O' Noodles cup
43. Dehydrated Stroganoff rehydrator
44. Bean soaker
45. Rice cooker
46. Overnight oats bowl
47. Peanut butter jar
48. Duct tape spool
49. Teapot
50. Wee firkin
51. Utensil holder
52. Soft-boiled-egg cooker
53. Gorp crock
54. Glühwein vessel
55. Egg scrambler
56. Pancake batter mixer
57. Lamp base
58. Bubble bath bottle

59. Poison oak scratch preventer (tape your hands to it)

60. Hot toddy tub

61. Dr. Bronner's soap supplier

62. Milk bottle

63. Dumbbell

64. Bowling pin

65. Hatstand

66. Headlamp holder

67. Smoothie sipper

68. Boot drier

69. Sock stretcher

70. Paintbrush holder

71. Watercolor rinse bucket

72. Treasure map case

73. Shish kebab skewer soaker

74. Kindling carrier

75. Licorice jar

76. Aromatherapy diffuser

77. Maple syrup pitcher

78. Button bin

79. Cord collector

80. Sugar canister

81. Orange juice carton

82. Short-lived sun shower

83. Berry basket

84. Cairn contributor

85. Gnome home

86. Arrowhead museum

87. Clothesline anchor

88. Buoy

89. Skipping stone dispenser

90. Coconut cracker

91. Kite weight

92. Porron, in a pinch

93. Cabasa

94. Cookie cutter (use the lid)

95. Salad dressing shaker

96. Sasquatch splasher

97. Seed saver

98. Hiccups mender

99. Imaginary friend

Around the Campfire

After the supper dishes are dried, s'mores fixings supplied, and mosquito repellent reapplied, it's time to gather round the fire for the evening program. Well-told ghost stories, interactive group games, and spirited sing-alongs will keep the fun going until your sleeping bags beckon or the camp host delivers a pointed reminder about quiet hours, whichever comes first.

Backcountry Crooning

Break out the ukuleles, harmonicas, and pan flutes and serenade the stars with robust renditions of these campfire-friendly classics.

"Linger"

"Do Your Ears Hang Low?"

"This Land Is Your Land"

"Home on the Range"

"Roll On, Columbia, Roll On"

"Oh! Susanna"

"John Jacob Jingleheimer Schmidt"

"On Top of Spaghetti"

"Kookaburra"

"Free to Be . . . You and Me"

"Moonshadow"

"Puff, the Magic Dragon"

"Raindrops Keep Fallin' on My Head"

"We Gotta Get Out of This Place"

Truth or Dare

Nothing bonds (or breaks up) a group like a game of truth or dare. The rules are simple: Choose one or the other, then answer the question or complete the dare. If you refuse, suffer the consequences predetermined by the group (e.g., chugging ginger beer, cast-iron-skillet-cleaning duty, sleeping right next to the bear locker). If you're having trouble thinking of prompts, here are a few examples.

Truth

- What's the funniest place you've peed outdoors?

- If you had to push one of us out of a canoe to keep it from sinking in giant-catfish-infested waters, who would it be?

- Did a raccoon really eat all the granola bars last night or was it *you*?

- What *exactly* is in this bug juice?

- Which one of us looks the sexiest in their camo-print napsack?

- Seeing as this ferocious freak thunderstorm shows no sign of letting up, and *someone* forgot the rainfly, would you swap your spouse (or parent, offspring, dog, wedding ring, Subaru Forester) for a luxury hotel suite right about now?

Dare

- Eat a chili-smothered s'more.

- Use the campground shower barefoot.

- Walk to the next campsite and ask to trade your yurt for their 45-foot luxury RV.

- Canoe across the lake using the pancake spatula in lieu of a paddle.

- Streak through Loop A.

- While streaking Loop A, pause at the camp host's site and ask him or her what time the hot yoga class starts at the campground amphitheater.

Firelight Fright

Come armed with your favorite tales from the crypt, such as "The Big Toe," "The Black Velvet Ribbon," and "Don't Turn On the Lights." Alter the story to give it a familiar and realistic setting (e.g., a dark forest, a remote cabin very much like the one you're staying in, or the ultra-creepy abandoned mill down the road from your campground), act anxious and jittery while you talk, and end with a sudden movement or sound. Should you have a flair for extemporaneous storytelling, you can always just wing it, or use this helpful Mad Libs–style ghost story template.

POST-DINNER PREDICAMENT

One _____ and _____ night, after they'd eaten
      (adjective)   *(adjective)*

a(n) _____ meal of _____ and _____,
    (synonym for amazing)   *(book recipe)*   *(book recipe)*

a bunch of campers sat down around the campfire.

Suddenly, they heard a(n) _____ from the nearby
                      (type of noise)

_____, and because they weren't very _____,
(place)   *(adjective)*

instead of calling the _____, they went to investigate.
           (noun)

They followed the sound deeper and deeper into the _____,
                      (same place as above)

until they came to a large _____.
           (new place)

A(n) _____ sight greeted their eyes—a(n) _____
    (synonym for terrifying)   *(scary adjective)*

had dragged _____ all the way from the camp kitchen and was
      (scary noun)

_____ it/them.
(verb, present participle)

After a(n) _____ and _____ struggle, the campers
      (adjective)   *(synonym for futile)*

_____. Their bodies were never found.
(verb, past tense)

The end.

Sleep tight and don't let the _____ bite!
           (least favorite forest creatures)

Stargazing for City Slickers

Amateur astronomers delight in a starry, starry night.

Tall + Dark = Handsome

For the clearest conditions, escape the city lights and head to high altitude, ideally at an International Dark Sky Park, a protected area designated as an exceptional nocturnal environment. Avoid stargazing under a full moon. It can diminish viewing possibilities, not to mention attract werewolves.

Righto, Galileo

Anyone can point out the three familiars—the Big Dipper, the Little Dipper, Orion's Belt—so why not wow with a lesser-known asterism? During prime camping season in the northern hemisphere, spot the Summer Triangle. At dusk, look for the brightest star in the eastern sky. That's the apex of the triangle, sparkly blue Vega of the constellation Lyra, the harp. Down and to the left shines Deneb of Cygnus, the swan. Farther down and to the right shines Altair of Aquila, the eagle. If you're still not seeing it, wait until midnight and look directly overhead. There it is!

A Decent Proposal

Plan your campout to coincide with the Perseid meteor shower, which peaks on August 12 or 13 each year, and offers up to one hundred meteors per hour from the comfort of your camp chair.

Save Yourself

To find the North Star, Polaris, look for the Big Dipper, draw a line through the two stars on the outer edge of its scoop, and follow that line toward the horizon. Polaris will appear as a fixed point that neither rises nor sets. Walk toward it to go north. (But you already knew that. We hope.)

Need Some Space?

Take advantage of celestial tech resources. Sign up for a text alert from NASA when the International Space Station is within view. Download a star map app to decode the sky simply by pointing at it with your smartphone. Purchase a tabletop telescope. Rewatch 1986's finest film, *SpaceCamp*.

Darling, Disaster!
10 Camping Crises Averted

Should your camping trip turn catastrophic, pop under your poncho and consult this handy guide.

1. Bears Be Gone
Dissuade ursine interference by setting up your camp kitchen, food storage, and tent 100 feet apart in a "Bear-muda Triangle," with the sleeping area upwind. Find a sturdy branch and hoist the food bag 12 feet up a tree, 6 feet away from the nearest climbable trunk. Now scour the area for bear bait—berry thickets, honey pots, Goldilocks—and remove temptations.

2. Cold Feet
If there's a chill in the air when it's time to turn in, place a hot water bottle (real, or rigged with boiling water and an empty Nalgene) in the foot of your sleeping bag. If that's not toasty enough, invest in a double sleeping bag or zip two sleeping bags together to create one. You can't beat body heat.

3. Morning Do
Should condensation put a damper on your nylon nirvana, improve ventilation by staking the fly farther from the canopy and reorienting your tent so that a breeze can blow under it. Ban all wet clothes and boots from the premises.

4. Fire Nonstarter
On the off chance that your fire simply won't start, search your supplies for surprisingly flammable bits and bobs: potato chips,

lint, dried orange peels, photos of your enemies, and (with caution!) hand sanitizer, whiskey, the map.

5. Mosquito Mayhem
Keep the bane of your summer existence at bay by tossing sage and rosemary onto the campfire, burning a boatload of citronella candles, wielding a battery-operated fan, eating garlic, wearing long pants, slathering on repellent, and recruiting all campers to stalk that elusive buzz in the tent.

6. Smokey the Bore
Should your vision of a cozy campfire be dashed by a burn ban, compensate by throwing a Lantern-Light Poker Night. Set up LED lanterns and fairy lights and gather around the picnic table with cozy lap blankets, extra hats and gloves, thermos cocktails (see page 162), camp stove–ready skillet s'mores (see page 138), poker chips, cards, and cash.

7. O, Spork
Forgot a mixing bowl? Toss salad in a (clean) garbage bag. Plate? Substitute a Frisbee. Cutlery? Whittle chopsticks. Napkin? Gather leaves. Cups? Pass the canteen. Pots and pans? Use foil. Food? Go home.

8. Impromptu Infirmary
When tent poles and marshmallow sticks start flying, anything can happen. Keep first-aid frequent fliers—tweezers, moleskin, Band-Aids, antiseptic wipes, alcohol pads, burn cream, ibuprofen, antacid, antidiarrheal, antihistamine,

EpiPen—at the ready, and purchase a pre-packed kit from a reputable outdoor supplier if you plan to be anywhere that potable water tablets or rehydration salts sound potentially useful.

9. Musty, Rusty, All-Out Fusty
In anticipation of future foibles, upon arriving home, take the time to air out the tent, wash all the gear, resupply the first-aid and cookery kits, reseason the cast-iron cookware, and make sure all items are clean and dry before storing. Although this is absolutely the last thing you want to do after a campout, it's the most important, as it's the only way to ensure that you'll ever go camping again.

10. Know When to Fold 'Em
In the rare, unfortunate case of an outdoor meltdown spurred by a run-in with a skunk, a heretofore-unseen-forehead-level branch, a monsoon, a hailstorm, a s'mores shortage, a capsized canoe, an ill-timed breakup, an inexplicable full-body rash, or the like, don't be afraid to pack it in. It is of the utmost importance to keep a satisfaction to stoicism ratio of 10:1, at minimum. That said, disasters make campouts memorable, so whenever possible, embrace the unexpected. Camping's fiercest foe, moodiness, can be easily staved off by stowing surprises (candy, trail mix, canteen cocktails) to reveal at just the right moment. Our trade secret? Always hide good candy in the glove box for the ride home.

5 Clever Camping Hacks

Since improvisation is the canny camper's best friend, here are five of our favorite handy hacks.

1. Camplifier
Hit Play on your music library, then drop your phone in a mug to simulate surround sound.

2. Headlamptern
Tape your headlamp to a Nalgene-style water bottle and let there be light.

3. Keeper of the Flame
Fill a mini Mason jar with matches, then affix a sandpaper circle to the lid to create your own fire starter.

4. Survival Set
Stuff an empty tin with a lighter, a pocketknife, a whistle, bandages, a compass, fishing line, and a wee bottle of Scotch. Just in case.

5. Swedish Torch
Craft a long-lasting fire with a built-in cooktop by tightly wiring six wedges of wood together using thin flexible wire. Stuff tinder in the center and light, for hours of slow burn.

The Ultimate Camp Kitchen

You'll be the envy of the entire campground when you break out this next-level camp kitchen, which has everything *and* the kitchen sink (with a gravity-fed faucet, of course). Hang the lantern, line up your Wüsthofs along the magnetic knife rack, organize the spice and silverware drawers, mix yourself a Vesper of the Valley (page 161), and start prepping the smashed potatoes.

What's in Your Backpack? The Definitive Packing List

Camp cooking is all the more enjoyable when you come bearing food, forks, and fire starters, so stock your station wagon with these backwoods brass tacks.

ESSENTIALS	EXTRAS
☐ Camp stove and propane	☐ "The Ultimate Camp Kitchen" (page 39)
☐ Firewood and hardwood charcoal	☐ Gravity-fed faucet
☐ Chimney starter	☐ Portable cocktail bar
☐ Matches or lighter	☐ Tablecloth
☐ Enamelware	☐ Hatchet
☐ Cutlery	☐ Teakettle
☐ Cooking utensils	☐ Insulated growler
☐ Foil	☐ Screen shelter
☐ Cast-iron Dutch oven	☐ Rolla Roasters (see page 23)
☐ Cast-iron skillet	☐ Pie irons
☐ Fireproof oven mitts	☐ Lid lifter
☐ Barbecue tongs	☐ Cast-iron drop-biscuit pan
☐ Wine and bottle openers	☐ Campfire claw
☐ Can opener	☐ Camp-cooking tripod
☐ Cutting board and knife	☐ Spit rotisserie
☐ Mixing bowls	☐ Meat thermometer
☐ Newspaper	☐ Grill grid
☐ Trash and storage bags	☐ Spice set
☐ Paper towels and dish towels	☐ First-aid kit
☐ Dish soap and sponge	☐ Fire extinguisher
☐ Antibacterial wipes	☐ Floss
☐ Food!	

Chapter 2

Trail Snacks

A generous supply of snacks can mean the difference between life and death when marching up and down mountains, across the great plains, over rushing rivers, or just from the car to the campsite—depending on how well your fellow campers cope with low blood sugar. Stay safe and keep your parka pockets, backpack, and picnic pantry well stocked with these irresistible grab-and-go goodies, designed to be made at home before the campout and revealed with a great flourish.

Gorgeous Gorp

Transcend good ol' raisins and peanuts in seven swift steps.

1. Pack Plenty
Bring 1 cup trail mix per camper, plus an extra cup for that errant enthusiast.

2. Prevent Picking
Trail mix goes off the rails when there's a lot of day-to-day filler (sad raisins) and just a little of that thing everyone wants (chocolate). Go big on the good stuff.

3. Scoop Like So
2 cups nuts, 1 cup crunch (seeds or grains or cereal), 1 cup dried fruit, 1 cup surprise, such as cacao nibs, candied ginger, or edible gold flakes.

4. Refresh Your Bulk-Bin Bounty
Toast nuts on a parchment paper–lined baking sheet in a 350°F oven for 8 to 15 minutes, tossing at least once, or in a skillet over medium heat for 3 to 5 minutes, tossing frequently, until fragrant and one shade darker.

5. Keep the Mix Colorful
Select diverse items to create visual je ne sais quoi, and package prettily. We hike with our feet and eat with our eyes.

6. Trust the Trifecta
Sweet, salty, spicy.

7. Choose Your Moment
There's a fine art to dishing out gorp just when your campers need it most. Nothing boosts morale like a well-timed M&M.

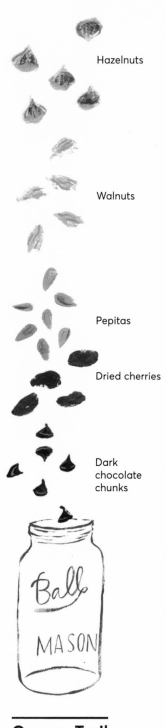

Hazelnuts

Walnuts

Pepitas

Dried cherries

Dark chocolate chunks

Oregon Trail

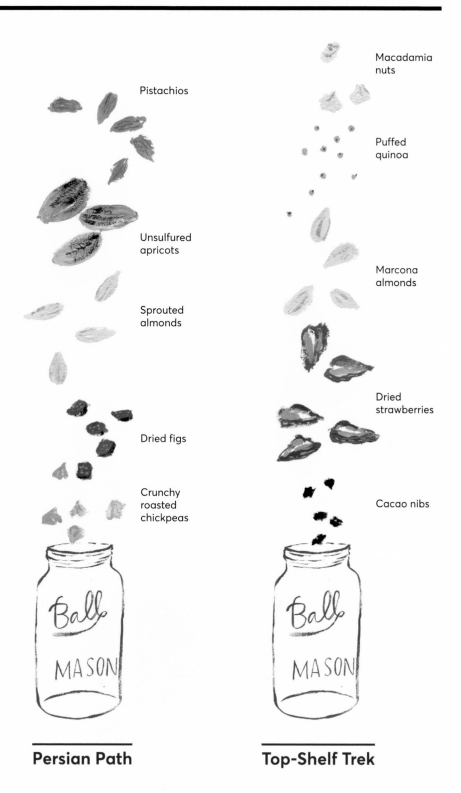

Pistachios

Macadamia
nuts

Puffed
quinoa

Unsulfured
apricots

Marcona
almonds

Sprouted
almonds

Dried figs

Dried
strawberries

Crunchy
roasted
chickpeas

Cacao nibs

Ball
MASON

Ball
MASON

Persian Path

Top-Shelf Trek

Pistachio Coconut Ginger Granola Bars

Besides a bear bell and wicking socks, there's no better hiking buddy than a good old-fashioned granola bar. We use brown rice syrup to bind these coconut-and-ginger-spiked snacks, because it produces a perfectly chewy bar with just the right amount of sweetness. **Makes 16**

2 tablespoons unsalted butter
1¼ cups rolled oats
½ cup unsweetened finely shredded coconut
¾ cup shelled roasted salted pistachios (see Tiny Tip)
½ cup roasted salted cashews
½ cup crispy rice cereal
¾ cup golden raisins
1½ teaspoons ground ginger
¼ teaspoon ground cardamom
¼ teaspoon kosher salt
½ teaspoon pure vanilla extract
½ cup brown rice syrup

tiny tip: If you're buying bulk-bin unshelled pistachios (amen for the bulk bins!), it takes just shy of 2 cups unshelled to equal ¾ cup shelled—that's 8 ounces if you're weighing, or a bag that's roughly the size of a large grapefruit if you're eyeballing.

1. Preheat the oven to 325°F. Line a 9-by-13-inch baking pan with parchment paper.

2. Melt the butter in a large skillet over medium heat. Mix in the oats and cook, stirring often, until they smell toasty and start to turn golden, 8 to 10 minutes. (If the oats quickly get too brown, lower the heat.) Add the coconut and stir until it's starting to brown, about 1 minute. Remove the pan from the heat and mix in the pistachios, cashews, cereal, golden raisins, ginger, cardamom, salt, and vanilla. Add the rice syrup and stir to combine.

3. Press the mixture into the prepared pan and pack firmly with a rubber spatula or wet fingers. Bake for 15 minutes, then remove from the oven and gently but firmly repack the top of the mixture with the spatula. Let cool completely, about 1 hour, then transfer to a cutting board and slice into sixteen 1½-by-4½-inch bars. Store the bars in an airtight container with parchment paper between the layers for up to 1 week at room temperature, or wrap them individually and freeze for up to 3 months.

Chocolate Cherry Chia Granola Bars

The trick to keeping the chocolate from melting into a (rather delightfully) gooey mess is to let the oat-almond mixture cool before mixing it in, but not so much that the brown rice syrup gets too sticky and stubborn to work with. Toss a few chocolate chunks into the mix as testers—if they stay mostly intact, you've hit the sweet spot. **Makes 16**

2 tablespoons unsalted butter
1½ cups rolled oats
1 cup coarsely chopped roasted almonds
¾ cup hulled raw unsalted sunflower seeds
2 tablespoons chia seeds
2 teaspoons ground cinnamon
½ teaspoon kosher salt
½ teaspoon pure vanilla extract
1 cup chopped dark sweet cherries (see Tiny Tip)
½ cup brown rice syrup
4 ounces dark chocolate (70% cacao or higher), chopped into ⅓-inch pieces

tiny tip: We enjoy an embarrassment of cherry riches in Oregon, and while we try not to play favorites, it's hard not to love the almighty Bing best. When dried, it's incomparably sweet-tart and chewy, perfect for these hearty bars.

1. Preheat the oven to 325°F. Line a 9-by-13-inch baking pan with parchment paper.

2. Melt the butter in a large skillet over medium heat. Mix in the oats and cook, stirring often, until they smell toasty and start to turn golden, 8 to 10 minutes. (If the oats quickly get too brown, lower the heat.) Remove the pan from the heat and mix in the almonds, sunflower seeds, chia seeds, cinnamon, salt, and vanilla, then mix in the cherries. Add the rice syrup and stir to combine. Let the mixture cool until a chunk of chocolate tossed into the mix stays mostly intact, 15 to 20 minutes. Quickly fold in the chocolate, press the mixture into the prepared pan, and pack it firmly with a rubber spatula or wet fingers.

3. Bake for 15 minutes, then remove from the oven and gently but firmly repack the top of the mixture with the spatula. Let cool completely, about 90 minutes, then transfer to a cutting board and slice into sixteen 1½-by-4½-inch bars. Store the bars in an airtight container with parchment paper between the layers for up to 1 week at room temperature, or wrap them individually and freeze for up to 3 months.

Cinnamon Sunbutter

When it comes time for a snappy snack, there's no denying the appeal of fresh fruits and veggies—from thickly sliced Honeycrisp apples to good old celery sticks. This healthy, lick-your-lips seed butter is ready for dunking, and offers a delicious alternative to nut butters for little dippers with allergies. **Makes 2 cups**

3 cups hulled roasted
   unsalted sunflower seeds
1 tablespoon ground
   cinnamon
1 tablespoon coconut oil
2 tablespoons honey
½ teaspoon kosher salt

1. In a food processor, grind the sunflower seeds until a smooth paste forms, 7 to 9 minutes, stopping occasionally to break up the mixture with a spatula if it clumps. Add the cinnamon, coconut oil, honey, and salt and process until silky smooth, 8 to 10 minutes (or less, if you prefer a coarser texture).

2. Transfer to two widemouthed 8-ounce Mason jars and store at room temperature for up to 1 week or refrigerate for up to 1 month.

MENU

Field and Stream Fête

Dig in to this midsummer night's dream dinner, which brings the finest from field and stream to the fire pit.

Golden Beet–Pickled Eggs 54

**Garden-Raid Tomato, Cucumber,
and Melon Salad** 83

Ember-Baked Rainbow Carrots and Baby Potatoes 74

Buttermilk Biscuits 208
with smoked honey

**Skillet-Fried Rainbow Trout
with Lemon and Fresh Dill** 124

Cherry Berry Slump 152

Vanilla Bourbon Hot Apple Cider 169

Old-Growth Evergreens Toddy 171

Slow 'n' Low Fruit Rolls, 4 Ways

You'll prep these chewy, richly flavored fruit snacks in a matter of minutes, but they'll take their sweet time in the oven, so plan this project for the day before your trip. When transferring the fruit purée to the baking sheet, aim for roughly ⅛ inch thickness in the middle and ¼ inch thickness on the sides to combat crispy edges. If the leather gets too dry and brittle at any point, brush it with water to revive it. And if the edges are done but the middle is dragging its fruity feet, pull out the tray, trim the edges with scissors, and set aside or nibble as a kitchen snack while the rest continues baking. **Makes 9 strips (per variation)**

Berry Beet
2 cups mixed berries, fresh or defrosted frozen
2 cups chopped steamed or roasted beets
2 tablespoons honey

Mango Chile Sesame
4 cups chopped mango
1 tablespoon sesame seeds
¼ teaspoon chipotle chile powder

Pineapple Coconut
4 cups chopped fresh pineapple
2 tablespoons honey
¼ cup unsweetened flaked coconut

Banana Maple Walnut
4 cups chopped ripe bananas (about 6 large bananas)
2 tablespoons maple syrup
2 tablespoons finely chopped walnuts

1. Preheat the oven to 175°F. Line a 12-by-18-inch rimmed baking sheet with parchment paper or a silicone baking mat (see Tiny Tip).

2. In a high-speed blender, purée the fruit and honey or maple syrup (if called for) until smooth, about 30 seconds. Transfer the purée to the baking sheet and smooth evenly with a spatula. If called for, sprinkle the nuts, seeds, or spices over the top. Bake until dry to the touch, about 4 hours.

3. Cool, line with parchment paper if you used a baking mat, and cut into 2-inch strips with scissors or a pizza cutter, then roll, and secure with kitchen twine. Store in an airtight container for up to 3 days at room temperature.

tiny tip: If you've been on the fence about buying silicone baking mats, now would be a good time to run to the nearest kitchenware shop—using a Silpat or other silicone baking mat makes baking fruit leather so much easier.

Cape Gooseberry Trail Mix

Nuts and dried fruit become the utmost gorgeous trail-fortifier when teensy, tart, antioxidant- and protein-packed Cape gooseberries join the pack. When eaten in tandem with sparkly candied ginger, they're nature's answer to Sour Patch Kids. (Our ultimate compliment.) **Makes 5 cups**

1 cup shelled raw pecans
1 cup shelled raw walnuts
1 cup shelled raw pepitas (pumpkin seeds)
1 cup unsweetened coconut flakes
2 tablespoons coconut oil, melted
2 tablespoons dark maple syrup
2 teaspoons pure vanilla extract
½ teaspoon orange blossom water
1 teaspoon kosher salt
⅓ cup cubed candied ginger
Sugar
1 cup dried Cape gooseberries (see Tiny Tip)

tiny tip: Cape gooseberries are also sold as Peruvian groundcherries, goldenberries, and Incaberries. You can find them at Whole Foods or your local co-op grocery. In a pinch, substitute dried cherries, golden raisins, dried blueberries, goji berries, or dried cranberries.

1. Preheat the oven to 350°F. Line a rimmed baking sheet with parchment paper.

2. Toss the pecans, walnuts, pepitas, and coconut flakes in a large bowl.

3. Whisk together the coconut oil, maple syrup, vanilla, orange blossom water, and salt in a small bowl. Pour over the nut mixture and toss with a rubber spatula until everything is coated. Spread in a single layer on the prepared baking sheet. Bake for 15 to 18 minutes, stirring midway through the baking time, until the coconut flakes and the nuts are toasted. Let cool completely and transfer to a large bowl.

4. In a small bowl, toss the candied ginger with a spoonful of sugar to coat the sticky cut sides. Remove the pieces with a slotted spoon and gently combine with the cooled nut mix and dried fruit.

5. Store in an airtight container for up to 2 weeks at room temperature, or divide into individual portions in cellophane bags.

Beerlao Nut Chow

Loaded with crisp lime leaves, salty nuts, and spicy chiles, this updated Chex mix—the fever dream of two Americans trekking through Southeast Asia—pairs best with a cold beer and freshly pried-off hiking boots. **Makes 9 cups**

2 cups Corn Chex cereal

2 cups Wheat Chex cereal

1 cup unsalted roasted peanuts

1 cup unsalted roasted cashews

3 cups checkerboard pretzels or pretzel sticks

1 ounce fresh makrut lime leaves (½ cup lightly packed; see Tiny Tip)

4 tablespoons (½ stick) unsalted butter, melted

¼ cup peanut oil

¼ cup packed light brown sugar

1 teaspoon finely grated fresh ginger

1 teaspoon garlic powder

½ teaspoon onion powder

2 tablespoons minced fresh lemongrass

2 teaspoons kosher salt

3 red bird's-eye chiles, thinly sliced (see Tiny Tip)

1. Position racks in the upper and lower thirds of the oven. Preheat the oven to 250°F. Line two rimmed baking sheets with parchment paper.

2. Toss together the Corn Chex, Wheat Chex, peanuts, cashews, pretzels, and lime leaves in a large bowl.

3. Whisk together the butter, peanut oil, brown sugar, ginger, garlic powder, onion powder, lemongrass, salt, and chiles in a large liquid measuring cup. Pour over the cereal mixture and toss with a rubber spatula until everything is coated.

4. Divide the mixture between the prepared baking sheets. Bake for 1 hour, stirring every 15 minutes and rotating the baking sheets halfway through. Cool completely and store in an airtight container for up to 1 week at room temperature.

tiny tip: Bird's-eye chiles and makrut lime leaves are available at Asian grocery stores, as well as online. In a pinch, substitute ½ teaspoon cayenne pepper for the chiles.

Furikake Flurry

The salt and pepper of Japan, *furikake*, and the prettiest of rice crackers, *arare*, unite in a mix that takes a cue from Hawaii's favorite surf camp treat, hurricane popcorn. Raid your local Asian market for the goods. **Makes 12 cups**

4 tablespoons (½ stick) unsalted butter
2 teaspoons sugar
1 teaspoon soy sauce
8 cups freshly popped popcorn (from ½ cup white popcorn kernels)
¼ cup nori komi furikake
1 cup roasted salted peanuts
2 cups arare (assorted bite-size Japanese rice crackers)
1 cup shelled roasted edamame (soybeans; see Tiny Tip)

1. Melt the butter in a small saucepan over low heat. Stir in the sugar and soy sauce until combined.

2. Put a layer of popcorn in a large lidded pot or paper bag, pour some of the butter mix over the top, and then sprinkle with furikake. Replace the lid and shake. Repeat with another layer until you've used up all the butter mix. Add the peanuts, arare, and roasted edamame and shake again. Store in an airtight container for up to 3 days at room temperature.

tiny tip: If you can't find shelled roasted edamame (soybeans), you can substitute wasabi peas.

Golden Beet–Pickled Eggs

This Pantone Yellow tri-purpose pickling project will yield a half dozen hard-boiled eggs for a protein-rich snack, briny beets for your Pioneer Picnic (page 66), *and* pretty pickled onions for the Sliced Tri-Tip Sandwich Bar (page 94). **Makes 6**

3 golden beets, scrubbed
(see Tiny Tip)
6 large eggs
½ white onion, thinly sliced
1 large garlic clove,
smashed
1 cup white wine vinegar
1 tablespoon kosher salt
1 tablespoon honey
2 teaspoons whole black
peppercorns
1 teaspoon cumin seeds
1 teaspoon mustard seeds
½ teaspoon ground
turmeric
1 cinnamon stick
1 bay leaf

tiny tip: If yellow really isn't your color, substitute red beets for the golden ones, and omit the turmeric. Or, to really brighten up the campsite, make a batch of each.

1. Preheat the oven to 400°F.

2. Wrap the beets in aluminum foil and roast until tender when pierced with a fork, 45 minutes to 1 hour. Unwrap the foil and let cool, then peel and cut each beet into 8 wedges.

3. Prepare an ice bath by filling a large bowl with water and ice, and bring a large saucepan of water to a boil. Using a slotted spoon, gently lower the eggs into the boiling water, then reduce the heat to maintain a low boil and cook for 13 minutes. Remove the eggs and immediately transfer them to the ice bath to cool (this will help prevent the unsightly gray halo hard-boiled yolks are prone to developing). Peel the eggs and put them in a 1-quart Mason jar with the beets, onion, and garlic clove.

4. Combine the vinegar, salt, honey, peppercorns, cumin seeds, mustard seeds, turmeric, cinnamon stick, bay leaf, and ½ cup water in a small saucepan and bring to a boil. Reduce the heat, cover, and simmer for 5 minutes. Remove from the heat, remove and discard the bay leaf, and pour the pickling brine into the jar over the eggs and vegetables. Secure the lid and firmly shake and twist to distribute the brine and spices. Let the jar cool to room temperature, then refrigerate and let everything marinate for at least 24 hours before eating. Store the eggs in their brine in the refrigerator for up to 1 month.

Smoked Trout Spread

Transform catch into canapés quicker than a fisherman can tell you about the weather conditions. **Makes 2 cups**

1 cup crème fraîche
2 tablespoons fresh lemon juice
1 tablespoon minced fresh tarragon, plus more for garnish
2 teaspoons capers, drained and rinsed
8 ounces smoked trout, skin removed
Kosher salt and freshly ground pepper
Cracked pepper crackers, toast points, or bagels, for serving

1. In a medium bowl, use a fork to combine the crème fraîche, lemon juice, tarragon, capers, and two-thirds of the trout. Mix until the fish is thoroughly incorporated in small flakes. Season with salt and pepper. Flake the remaining trout in handsome, larger flakes and stir into the dip.

2. Pack into a lidded jar and garnish with tarragon. Serve with cracked pepper crackers or toast points, or on a bagel for breakfast.

Zhug Dip and Sweet Potato Chips

Is it possible to have a super-spicy relationship that's also good for you? Absolutely, when cilantro and parsley team up with zippy peppers and creamy yogurt in a gloriously green dip inspired by the Yemenite hot sauce *zhug*. Serve with impressively orange sweet potato chips (cooked on low heat to play up their head-turning looks) and colorful crudités for a pinup of a snack. **Makes 2 cups dip and 30 chips**

Chips
2 sweet potatoes
2 tablespoons coconut oil
Fine sea salt

Dip
Seeds from 4 green
    cardamom pods
1 teaspoon cumin seeds
1 cup lightly packed fresh
    cilantro
1 cup lightly packed fresh
    flat-leaf parsley
4 red bird's-eye chiles,
    coarsely chopped
2 serrano peppers,
    stemmed and seeded
4 garlic cloves
2 tablespoons fresh lemon
    juice
1 teaspoon kosher salt
¼ teaspoon freshly ground
    pepper
⅓ cup extra-virgin olive oil
1 cup plain full-fat Greek
    yogurt

1. To make the chips: Preheat the oven to 225°F. Line two baking sheets with parchment paper.

2. Peel the sweet potatoes and cut them lengthwise into 1/16-inch slices using a mandoline. Place them in a large bowl with the coconut oil and toss with your hands. Arrange the slices in a single layer on the prepared baking sheets, running each slice between your fingers to evenly coat with the oil. Reserve any slices that do not fit on the sheets.

3. Sprinkle lightly with sea salt and bake for 1 hour, rotating the baking sheets and flipping the slices every 15 minutes. Transfer to a cooling rack to crisp. Repeat with any sweet potato slices that did not fit. Cool completely and transport in a gallon-size resealable bag.

Crudités

½ small head Romanesco, divided into small florets

1 bunch purple carrots, scrubbed and halved lengthwise

2 bunches breakfast radishes

In the Backpack

☐ Large board or platter

4. To make the dip: Toast the cardamom and cumin seeds in a small sauté pan over medium heat until fragrant. Finely grind the spices using a mortar and pestle or spice grinder. Combine with the cilantro, parsley, chiles, serrano peppers, garlic, lemon juice, salt, and black pepper in a food processor and pulse until smooth, scraping the bowl as needed. With the motor running, add the olive oil in a stream, then add the yogurt and pulse until fully incorporated. Pack in a widemouthed pint jar, which will double as your serving dish.

5. To make the crudités: Before the campout, steam the Romanesco for 3 minutes, shock in a bowl of ice water, and tuck in the cooler in an airtight container. Scrub and trim the radishes and carrots and pack in an airtight container with a damp paper towel.

6. At the campout, arrange the Romanesco, carrots, radishes, and chips on a large board or platter and serve with the dip.

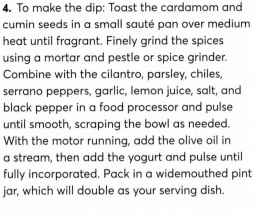

Figgy Pecan Crackers and Whipped Feta

Keep a little loaf of this wholesome seed bread in the freezer, and when a campout arises, slice and bake it into champion cheese-plate crackers to serve with a feta dip that comes together in less than five minutes (or with your favorite bloomy-rind cheese). **Makes 24 crackers and 1½ cups dip**

Crackers
Butter, for greasing
1 cup all-purpose flour, plus more for dusting
1 cup rye flour
2 teaspoons kosher salt
1 teaspoon baking soda
½ teaspoon ground cloves
½ teaspoon ground ginger
½ teaspoon ground cinnamon
1 cup buttermilk
⅓ cup honey
½ cup pecans, finely chopped
½ cup dried Mission figs, finely diced
2 tablespoons black chia seeds
¼ cup hulled sunflower seeds

1. To make the crackers: Preheat the oven to 350°F. Grease a loaf pan with butter and dust with flour, tapping out any excess.

2. Sift together the all-purpose flour, rye flour, salt, baking soda, cloves, ginger, and cinnamon into a medium bowl.

3. In the bowl of a stand mixer fitted with the paddle attachment, mix the buttermilk and honey on medium speed until combined. Add the flour mixture ½ cup at a time until just incorporated. Reduce the speed and gently stir in the pecans, figs, chia seeds, and sunflower seeds.

4. Transfer the dough to the prepared loaf pan and bake for 40 minutes, or until a toothpick inserted into the center comes out clean. Cool completely and, for the easiest slicing technique, wrap the loaf in plastic wrap and freeze until solid.

5. When ready to make the crackers, preheat the oven to 300°F. Line two baking sheets with parchment paper.

6. Remove the bread from the freezer and unwrap. Thinly slice the bread into ⅛-inch-thick rectangles. Divide the slices between the prepared baking sheets, keeping any thicker

Dip

8 ounces feta cheese,
   at room temperature
4 ounces cream cheese,
   at room temperature
3 tablespoons extra-virgin
   olive oil
1 teaspoon fresh lemon
   juice
¼ teaspoon freshly ground
   pepper
1 teaspoon fresh lemon-
   thyme leaves
Grated lemon zest, from
   half a lemon

pieces together. Bake for 20 to 30 minutes, until toasted and crispy (pull the sheet of thinner crackers first). Store in an airtight container at room temperature and eat within 2 weeks.

7. To make the dip: Combine the feta, cream cheese, 2 tablespoons of the olive oil, the lemon juice, and the pepper in a food processor and blend until silky smooth, 3 to 5 minutes. Transfer the whipped feta to a widemouthed jar. Sprinkle with the lemon-thyme leaves and lemon zest and drizzle with the remaining 1 tablespoon olive oil. Serve at room temperature with the crackers.

Smoky Spicy Salmon Jerky

In the Pacific Northwest, we're always looking for excuses to eat more of the superlative salmon the region is known for, and this tender, smoky-sweet jerky fits the bill. As an added bonus, it's even more delicious than conventional jerky, and it's refreshingly free of the preservatives, nitrates, and fillers often found in it. Let the salmon sit in the freezer for an hour or so prior to slicing; it'll be much easier to work with. **Serves 4**

1 cup soy sauce

¼ cup packed dark brown sugar

2 tablespoons fresh lemon juice

1 tablespoon freshly ground pepper

1 teaspoon liquid smoke

1 tablespoon hot sauce

1½ pounds skin-on salmon fillet, pin bones removed

1. Line two rimmed baking sheets with parchment paper and place wire racks on top.

2. Combine the soy sauce, brown sugar, lemon juice, pepper, liquid smoke, and hot sauce in a medium bowl.

3. Slice the salmon into ¼-inch-thick strips and transfer to a 1-gallon resealable plastic bag. Pour the marinade into the bag, seal it, and turn the bag, massaging to mix well. Let the salmon soak in the refrigerator for at least 4 hours, but preferably overnight, turning occasionally to evenly distribute the marinade.

4. Preheat the oven to 175°F.

5. Remove the salmon from the refrigerator. Arrange the strips of salmon on the prepared racks and discard the marinade. Bake until cooked through, dry to the touch, and tender-chewy, 2 to 3 hours. Let cool, transfer to an airtight container, and store at room temperature for up to 1 week.

Bulgogi Beef Jerky

Nuts and berries are the tried-and-true trail snack Trojans, but sometimes you crave something a little . . . *meatier*. Enter this Korean-spiced beef jerky, which takes a leisurely soak in a marinade infused with garlic, ginger, and pear before baking. For easier slicing, pop the beef in the freezer a few hours beforehand. (Just don't accidentally let it freeze solid; speaking from experience, this will put a real crimp in your jerky-making plans.)
Serves 4

Galbi Marinade
¾ cup soy sauce
⅓ cup toasted sesame oil
¼ cup pear juice
12 large garlic cloves, smashed
½ large onion, thinly sliced
6 green onions, coarsely chopped
2 tablespoons packed light brown sugar
2 teaspoons grated fresh ginger
2 teaspoons freshly ground pepper

2 pounds lean beef, such as top round or eye of round

1. Line two rimmed baking sheets with parchment paper and place wire racks on top.

2. To make the marinade: Combine the soy sauce, sesame oil, pear juice, garlic, sliced onion, green onions, brown sugar, ginger, and pepper in a large bowl.

3. Slice the beef against the grain into ¼-inch-thick strips. Transfer to a 1-gallon resealable plastic bag. Pour the marinade into the bag, seal it, and turn the bag, massaging to mix well. Let the beef soak in the refrigerator for at least 4 hours, but preferably overnight, turning occasionally to evenly distribute the marinade.

4. Preheat the oven to 175°F.

5. Remove the beef from the refrigerator. Arrange the strips of beef on the prepared racks and discard the marinade. Bake until cooked through, dry to the touch, and perfectly chewy, 3 to 4 hours. Let cool, transfer to an airtight container, and store at room temperature for up to 1 week.

Camping with Your Canine

We asked emergency medicine veterinarian Jenica Wycoff, who's camped all over the West with her one-eyed rescue dog, Bones, for details on making it in the wilderness with your not-so-wild animal.

Readiness Is All

Talk to your veterinarian to troubleshoot any site-specific preventative measures (e.g., vaccinating against rattlesnake bites), and prepare a canine first-aid kit to take with you. Add phone numbers for ASPCA Poison Control and your veterinarian to your contacts, and snap a photo of your dog's vaccination record, just in case.

Cool = Calm and Collected

Be aware of your dog's limits, because he likely isn't. ER vets see a lot of heatstroke in brachycephalic breeds especially. Offer your pug unlimited access to water and shut down his frantic exploration of the campground before he's too hot to trot.

Call of the Wild Animal Attacks

Should your dog have a run-in with wildlife, yell, whistle, or throw objects at the scuffle. Never physically intervene.

Flight Risk

Dogs run when they're scared, so if your dog seems anxious, keep him on a leash. To help him de-stress, provide familiar objects that smell like home (such as bedding) and consider purchasing an anti-anxiety vest.

Wild Strife

Call Poison Control immediately if your dog ingests mushrooms, poison ivy/oak, blue-green algae in standing water, rotting carcasses, fetid food, or marijuana or other recreational drugs.

De-Skunking: A Recipe

When man's best friend has a run-in with nose's worst enemy, whip up a batch of this odor-abating shampoo: 1 quart 3% hydrogen peroxide + ¼ cup baking soda + 1 teaspoon liquid soap.

The Prepared Pup

- Collar and ID tags
- Doggles (to prevent ocular trauma at windy campsites, such as Great Sand Dunes National Park and Preserve)
- Panniers
- Booties (to protect against hot and cold surfaces)
- Water bowl

Winnie's Biscuits

We created this buckwheat dog treat for our canine camping companion, a massive Bernese mountain dog whose enthusiastic appetite and touchy tummy can lead to some rather astounding tent toots. Loaded with stomach-soothing pumpkin, this protein-rich cookie is a real tail-wagger. We hope your pup loves it as much as Winnie does. **Makes twenty-four 3-inch dog bones or forty-eight 1½-inch hearts**

2 large eggs
One 15-ounce can pure
  pumpkin purée
½ cup natural peanut
  butter (see Tiny Tip)
1½ cups buckwheat flour,
  plus more for dusting
1½ cups fine-ground
  cornmeal
½ cup ground flaxseed

tiny tip: Read the peanut butter label—additives make pups sick.

1. Position racks in the upper and lower thirds of the oven. Preheat the oven to 350°F. Line two baking sheets with parchment paper.

2. In the bowl of a stand mixer fitted with the paddle attachment, mix the eggs, pumpkin purée, and peanut butter. Turn off the mixer, add the buckwheat flour, cornmeal, and ground flaxseed, and mix on low speed until the dough starts to pull away from the sides of the bowl. The dough will be very sticky. Divide the dough into 2 pieces, flatten into discs, and wrap in plastic wrap. Freeze for 30 minutes for easier handling.

3. Generously sprinkle the counter with buckwheat flour and transfer the dough onto it. Sprinkle the dough with more flour and use a rolling pin to roll it out to a ¼-inch thickness. Cut into shapes with a flour-dipped cookie cutter and transfer to the prepared baking sheets.

4. Bake until the biscuits are hard and dry, about 45 minutes. Cool completely, toss one to your eagerly awaiting pup, and pack the rest in a biscuit tin. The treats will keep at room temperature for up to 1 week and in the freezer for a season.

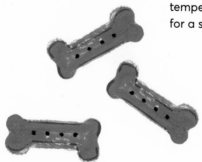

Chapter 3

Sides and Salads

Behind (or next to) every great hunk of grilled meat or coal-baked casserole, there should be a stunning side dish, be it a skillet of sweet-and-spicy Green Chile and Cheese Cast-iron Cornbread or a platter of tender, slightly smoky Grilled Little Gems with Cherry Tomatoes, Nectarines, and Creamy Dill Dressing. Whether you've got the cast-iron baking bug, a farmers' market haul that's ready for action, or a tomato bed that's reached maximum capacity and then some, here are plenty of ideas to keep the campsite picnic table heaped high with fresh, flavorful sides and salads.

Pioneer Picnic

Had the earliest campers in the great American outdoors been privy to today's splendid specialty markets, we'd like to think they would have circled their wagons around this grab-and-go supper spread.

- Summer sausage
- Aged Gouda
- Honeycrisp apples
- Blackberries
- A baguette
- Nuts

- Cornichons
- Pickled cauliflower
- Golden Beet–Pickled Eggs (page 54)
- Dark chocolate

Forest Fondue

Oozy, boozy coal-baked Camembert kicks off a forest fantasy meal when the teensy skillet hits the picnic table. If a Lilliputian pan is eluding you, securely wrap the cheese in several layers of heavy-duty foil instead.
Serves 4

One 8-ounce wheel
   Camembert cheese,
   or other bloomy-rind
   wheel of cheese
½ pear
2 tablespoons pear brandy
   (see page 217 for sources)
2 tablespoons finely
   chopped roasted
   hazelnuts
1 sprig fresh rosemary,
   for garnish
Sliced crusty bread,
   for serving

In the Backpack

- ☐ 6½-inch cast-iron skillet
- ☐ Cutting board
- ☐ Foil

Variation

Replace the pear with a handful of fresh blackberries or pitted and halved cherries to make Berry Brie Jamboree.

1. Prepare a campfire (see page 24) and fit it with a grill grate.

2. Line a mini (6½-inch) cast-iron skillet with foil, leaving enough overhang to create a foil packet. Place the Camembert inside and score the top with an X.

3. Place the pear half on a cutting board cut-side down and cut it into thin slices, keeping one end intact. Place your palm atop it, and gently rotate to fan the slices. Pop the pear fan on the cheese, douse the whole thing with the brandy, and crimp the foil to seal. Place the skillet on the fire pit grate or directly on coals, whichever is offering gentle, steady heat, and melt the cheese for 10 minutes or so. (Trust your nose. When the cheese is irresistibly gooey and smells stinky in the best way, you'll know it's ready.)

4. Remove from the heat and open the foil or, if you're a glutton for aesthetics as we are, tear off the foil from below as well, so the Camembert sits directly in the warm skillet. Sprinkle with the hazelnuts and garnish with the rosemary sprig. Dip bits of bread into the oozy cheese.

Garlicky Grilled Artichokes

In our formative camping years, grilled artichokes were the signature of a well-considered outdoor party, and we'll never shake that association. Arrive at the campground with these garlicky greenies pre-steamed and swimming in a plucky marinade, making them an exemplary appetizer to throw on the campfire grill just as soon as things heat up. **Serves 4**

Artichokes
4 medium artichokes
1 lemon, halved
Kosher salt

Marinade
3 garlic cloves, smashed
¾ cup extra-virgin olive oil
½ cup white balsamic vinegar
1 teaspoon kosher salt
½ teaspoon freshly ground pepper

Camping Aioli
Mayonnaise, preferably Best Foods or Hellmann's

In the Backpack

☐ Barbecue tongs

At Home
1. To make the artichokes: Lop off the top third of the artichoke using a sharp chef's knife. Snap off the toughest, outermost leaves and, using kitchen shears, snip off the thorny tips of the remaining leaves. Keep the stem long and trim a nickel-width from the end. Rub the freshly exposed bits with lemon. Repeat with the rest. Put a big pinch of salt and the juice of the lemon in a large pot, place a steaming basket inside it, and fill the pot with water to reach just under the basket. Set the artichokes inside, tails up.

2. Cover the pot and steam until the leaves are easily plucked and tender and the stem is easily pierced with a knife, about 25 minutes. Once the artichokes are cool enough to handle, transfer to a cutting board. Quarter each one lengthwise and remove the prickly choke from the heart using a paring knife and a spoon.

3. To make the marinade: Combine the garlic, olive oil, vinegar, salt, and pepper in a gallon-size resealable bag and add the artichokes. Seal the bag well.

At the Campout
4. Prepare a campfire (see page 24) and fit it with a grill grate.

5. Grill the artichokes over high heat for 10 minutes, turning so that marks appear on both faces. Serve with store-bought mayonnaise, er, Camping Aioli.

Sautéed Chanterelle Mushrooms

Besides the spectacular foliage and mild temperatures, autumn camping in Oregon comes with an added bonus—misty forests teeming with wild golden chanterelles, our state mushroom. It doesn't take much to turn these gilled gems into a showstopping side; a quick sauté with butter and herbs will do it, and if you also want to add a splash of cream, you won't be disappointed. If it isn't chanterelle season, substitute a mix of wild mushrooms, such as hedgehog, porcini, enoki, oyster, or hen-of-the-woods. **Serves 4**

1 tablespoon Shallot-Herb Butter (page 130)
1 tablespoon extra-virgin olive oil
1 pound chanterelle mushrooms, cleaned and torn into bite-size lengths (see Tiny Tip)
1 tablespoon sherry
2 teaspoons finely chopped fresh flat-leaf parsley

In the Backpack

☐ 12-inch cast-iron skillet

At Home

1. Prepare the Shallot-Herb Butter and refrigerate.

At the Campout

2. Prepare a campfire (see page 24).

3. Heat a 12-inch cast-iron skillet in the fire until hot but not smoking. Add the olive oil and butter and swirl to mix. Add the mushrooms and cook for 2 minutes. Add the sherry and cook, stirring occasionally, until the mushrooms are tender and dark golden brown, 7 to 10 minutes. Remove the skillet from the heat, sprinkle the chanterelles with the parsley, and serve.

---

tiny tip: If setting out on a chanterelle-hunting expedition, be sure to take along an experienced forager to avoid any run-ins with toxic impostors, such as those on page 81.

Corn on the Cob with Chili-Lime Butter

Soaking sweet summer corn in its husk before placing it in the campfire coals creates the perfect storm of steam and heat, giving you tender, juicy kernels with minimal effort. Plus, the husk handle gives diners a firm grip, so there's no need to pack the decorative corn holders. **Serves 6**

Chili-Lime Butter
   (page 130)
6 ears of corn, husks on
4 ounces cotija cheese,
   crumbled

In the Backpack

☐ Kitchen twine

☐ Bowl or bucket

☐ Barbecue tongs

tiny tip: Should a burn ban be in place, make cooler corn: Husk each ear completely; place all the ears in a clean, empty cooler, cover with water boiled on the propane stove, and close the lid. In 30 minutes, you should have perfectly cooked corn and a wilderness hack to remember.

At Home

1. Prepare the Chili-Lime Butter and refrigerate.

At the Campout

2. Prepare a campfire (see page 24).

3. Remove the Chili-Lime Butter from the cooler and let it come to room temperature. Carefully peel the corn husks away from the kernels without tearing them off, and remove and discard the corn silk. Replace the husk and use kitchen twine to tie it shut. Repeat with all 6 ears. Soak the trussed cobs in a large bowl or bucket of fresh cold water for 20 minutes.

4. Shake off the excess water from the corn and place the ears directly in the coals. Bake until cooked through, about 20 minutes, turning once. Remove from the coals and peel back the husks completely so that a handle forms, then slather the corn with Chili-Lime Butter and sprinkle with cotija.

Smoky Smashed Potatoes

Only good can come of combining four of the most heavenly foods known to (wo)man: potatoes, butter, bacon, and cheese. Dish these up alongside grilled steak, pork chops, or portobellos, and if at all humanly possible, save some for building breakfast burritos the next morning. **Serves 4**

Smoked Paprika–Garlic
  Butter (page 130)
1 pound small Yukon Gold
  potatoes
Kosher salt
8 ounces sliced bacon,
  cut crosswise into
  ½-inch-wide pieces
3 ounces grated smoked
  cheddar cheese
Freshly ground pepper

In the Backpack

☐ Large pot for boiling
  the potatoes
☐ 12-inch cast-iron skillet
☐ Foil (optional)
☐ Slotted spoon and
  spatula

At Home

1. Prepare the Smoked Paprika–Garlic Butter and refrigerate.

At the Campout

2. Prepare a campfire (see page 24) and fit it with a grill grate. Set up the camp stove.

3. Remove the Smoked Paprika–Garlic Butter from the cooler and let it come to room temperature. In a large pot over high heat on the camp stove, boil the potatoes in assertively salted water until fork-tender, 20 to 25 minutes.

4. While the potatoes are boiling, heat a 12-inch cast-iron skillet on the campfire grill grate or over medium-high heat on the camp stove and cook the bacon until crispy. With a slotted spoon, remove the bacon from the pan and set aside on a paper towel–lined plate. Pour all but 2 tablespoons of the bacon fat out of the skillet.

5. Drain the boiled potatoes and place them in the hot skillet. Use a spatula to gently but firmly smash each one down to about 1 inch thick. Spoon Smoked Paprika–Garlic Butter evenly over the top of the potatoes, then sprinkle with the cheddar and bacon and season with salt and pepper.

6. Place the skillet on the campfire grill, cover with a lid or foil, and cook until the potatoes are soft, sizzling, and melty, about 15 minutes. (Check the bottoms occasionally to prevent burning.) Season with salt and pepper and serve.

Hasselbackpack Potatoes

It's happened to every camp cook: a humble russet enters the coals longing to become a star side dish and emerges a scorched meteorite. Avoid that fate, and turn your potato into an applaudable accompaniment by prepping and parbaking your spud at home. **Serves 6**

6 medium Yukon Gold
  potatoes
2 tablespoons olive oil
2 teaspoons kosher salt
¾ teaspoon freshly ground
  pepper
6 ounces blue cheese,
  crumbled

In the Backpack

☐ Barbecue tongs

At Home

1. Preheat the oven to 350°F.

2. Set two wooden spoons on a cutting board and rest a potato between the handles. Cut crosswise into ¼-inch-thick slices, using the spoon handle guides to stop just short of slicing through the bottom of the potato. Repeat with all the potatoes. Combine the olive oil, salt, and pepper in a small bowl and work the mixture into each potato's slats. Place on a baking sheet and bake for 30 minutes, until the potatoes are not quite tender.

3. Once the potatoes are cool enough to handle, stuff 1 ounce of the crumbled blue cheese between the slats of each potato. Double wrap each potato in foil and transport in a cooler filled with ice.

At the Campout

4. Prepare a bed of hardwood charcoal (see page 24).

5. Bury the wrapped potatoes in the coals until the cheese is melty and the potatoes are fork-tender, about 30 minutes, turning halfway through with tongs. Unveil a dreamy spud that's deserving of a Big Sky Rib-Eye (page 132).

Foil Packet Primer

It's only natural to reach for your trusty, nonrusty (see page 27) cast iron when a supper situation arises. But plain old aluminum foil has its place in the coals, too, as you may well remember from your summer camp days, when ground beef and chopped bell pepper packets were all the alfresco mess-hall rage. Before you start your steam engines, read these five packet principles.

1. Build a Better Steam Trap

Since the contents of a foil packet cook via steam, make sure you've provided moisture (in the form of wine, miso, coconut milk, tears of joy, etc.), then make sure the moisture stays put with a forceful fold. Depending on your meal's mass, lay out 12 to 18 inches of heavy-duty foil (or double-layer regular foil) per packet, then position the ingredients in the center, leaving enough room for an air pocket. Bring the short ends together and fold over twice, then tightly fold (don't crumple) in the loose ends to seal the deal.

2. Dress in Layers

Meat is best positioned on the bottom of the packet, since it must be cooked through, for reasons of both safety and satisfaction. Delicate fresh herbs, minced garlic, and cheese are the most vulnerable to scorching, so when constructing your packet, keep them toward the top. Add liquids and fats last, so that they'll slowly mix and mingle with everything on their way down.

3. Coal-bal Positioning

Before plopping down your packets, build up a nice thick bed of coals (about 2 inches) that follow the Goldilocks principle: neither too hot (bright red) nor too cold (a tepid black), but just right (grayish white means go). Ward off hot spots by rotating the packets halfway through the cooking time. The average foil packet takes 20 to 30 minutes to cook, but as always, use your best judgment, and reevaluate at the first whiff of burnt Broccolini. When in doubt, get the cabbage out, and line the packet with a leaf on the top and bottom as insulation. Speaking of insulation, handle hot packets with oven mitts and unfurl them carefully to avoid steam burns.

4. Smorgaspacket

Besides being fast and unfussy, packet possibilities are virtually limitless, so finicky eaters and adventurous epicureans, vegans and carnivores, can stuff and steam alongside each other in perfect harmony. Prep a dozen or so ingredients at home, transport in resealable deli containers, then let the group mix and match.

5. Tinfoil Toss

Last, let's consider what is possibly foil packets' most significant advantage: zero cleanup required. Just lick the foil clean, crumple it into a ball, and compete to see who can recycle their former Tinfoil Shrimp Boil (page 121) from the fire pit free-throw line. Winner gets the first S'moopwafel (page 139).

From Farm to Fire: Ember-Baked Accompaniments

When the farmers' market's finest meet foil and fire, it's the beginning of a beautiful friendship. These herbivore-approved medleys have five ingredients or fewer, so they're light on prep and heavy on flavor. Simply fold everything into a double-layer foil pouch, set it on the campfire coals (or on a grate directly above it), rotate periodically, and wait, preferably while sipping ice-cold *tepache*. Voilà—hot and steamy ready-to-serve sides.

	1 bunch **rainbow carrots**, halved and split + 2 tablespoons Maple Bourbon Butter (see page 204) + 2-inch strip orange zest (15 minutes)
	1 pound **baby potatoes** + 2 tablespoons whole-grain mustard + ¼ cup white wine vinegar + 2 slices uncooked bacon, chopped (30 minutes)
	1 bunch **Japanese turnips**, halved + 2 tablespoons Shallot-Herb Butter (page 130) + 2 tarragon sprigs (20 minutes)
	1 bunch **red beets**, trimmed and scrubbed + 1 tablespoon grated fresh horseradish + 2 tablespoons red wine vinegar + ½ teaspoon caraway seeds (40 minutes)
	2 large **sweet potatoes**, peeled and cubed + 3 curry leaves + ¼ cup coconut milk + 1 green cardamom pod (20 minutes)

	1 pint **cherry tomatoes** + 2 smashed garlic cloves + 3 oregano sprigs + 1 tablespoon olive oil (20 minutes)
	1 head **cauliflower**, broken into florets + 1 tablespoon harissa + ¼ cup pitted oil-cured olives + ¼ cup olive oil + ¼ cup finely grated Parmigiano-Reggiano, to finish (15 minutes)
	1 pound **cipollini onions** + 2 tablespoons sherry vinegar + 3 thyme sprigs + ¼ teaspoon cracked black peppercorns (15 minutes)
	1 pound **Brussels sprouts**, halved + ½ cup spicy kimchi + 2 tablespoons kimchi brine + 1 teaspoon grated fresh ginger (20 minutes)
	1 pound **shishito peppers** + 1 tablespoon miso paste mashed with 2 tablespoons unsalted butter + ¼ cup mint leaves (20 minutes)
	6 pitted **apricots** + 2 tablespoons honey + 1 small sprig rosemary + ¼ cup St-Germain elderflower liqueur (15 minutes)
	1 quart **strawberries**, hulled + 1 tablespoon balsamic vinegar + 1 teaspoon pure vanilla extract + 2 tablespoons brown sugar (15 minutes)

Bacon Molasses Baked Beans

Complete the camp-food trifecta (alongside hot dogs and marshmallows, of course) with slow-cooked baked beans, prepared at home and reheated over the fire. Spoon these Boston beauties atop a coal-baked potato, ladle them onto a plate with a roasted frank, or dish them solo as a soul-satisfying bowl following a day in the woods. **Makes 8 cups**

1 pound dried navy beans
Kosher salt
1 bay leaf
½ cup dark molasses
2 teaspoons dry mustard
1 teaspoon freshly ground
   pepper
8 ounces slab bacon,
   thinly sliced
1 medium onion, minced
4 cups chicken stock
2 tablespoons cider vinegar

In the Backpack

☐ 10-inch cast-iron
   Dutch oven
☐ Ladle

At Home

1. Rinse the beans and pluck out the uglies. Soak the beans overnight in a large bowl or pot with 1 tablespoon salt and enough water to cover by a few inches. Drain the beans and place in a Dutch oven with the bay leaf and cool water to cover by a few inches. Bring to a boil and reduce the heat to maintain a simmer. Put on the lid and simmer, stirring now and again, until the beans are cooked through, about 1 hour. Drain the beans, reserving the bean bath.

2. Preheat the oven to 325°F.

3. Whisk 2 cups of the bean bath with the molasses, dry mustard, pepper, and 1 teaspoon salt in a medium bowl.

4. Cook the bacon in a large Dutch oven over medium-high heat until the fat begins to render, then add the onion and cook for 5 minutes. Add the drained beans, the molasses mixture, and the stock. Cover and bake for 2½ hours, occasionally adding more bean bath (and, if that runs out, boiling water) to keep the beans covered. Remove the lid, stir, season with salt and pepper, and bake, uncovered, for 1 hour more, until a deep-brown crust forms. Stir, check the seasoning, discard the bay leaf, and finish with the vinegar. Transfer to a resealable container and transport in a cooler filled with ice.

At the Campout

5. Prepare a campfire (see page 24) or set up the camp stove.

6. In a 10-inch cast-iron Dutch oven, reheat the beans over low heat, stirring occasionally to prevent dreaded burnt-bean bottom. Serve piping hot.

Roasted Garlic Parmesan Monkey Bread

Serve these soft, chewy, roasted-garlic-butter-drenched dough balls as a side, or serve them solo, with Rucksack Red Sauce (page 100) and Creamy Dill Dressing (see page 79) for dipping. **Serves 6**

Perfect Pizza Dough
(page 101)
Spicy Roasted Garlic Butter
(page 130)
2 ounces grated Parmesan
cheese, preferably
Parmigiano-Reggiano
1 tablespoon finely
chopped fresh flat-leaf
parsley
½ teaspoon red pepper
flakes

In the Backpack

☐ 12-inch cast-iron
Dutch oven

At Home

1. Prepare the Perfect Pizza Dough. Reserve half for the monkey bread and half for another use (or a second batch of monkey bread). Prepare the Spicy Roasted Garlic Butter and refrigerate. Combine the Parmigiano-Reggiano, parsley, and red pepper flakes in a 1-pint Mason jar, shake to mix, and refrigerate.

At the Campout

2. Prepare a campfire (see page 24) and, if using, set up the camp stove.

3. Melt the Spicy Roasted Garlic Butter in a small saucepan over the campfire or low camp stove heat. Divide the pizza dough into 24 pieces. Roll each piece in the melted butter, then nestle it in an even layer into a 12-inch cast-iron Dutch oven. Pour the remaining butter over the top, put on the lid, and let rise in a warm spot until the dough doubles in size, about 45 minutes.

4. Sprinkle the dough with the cheese mixture, then replace the lid. Bake at 375°F (9 hot coals under the Dutch oven, 16 on the lid) until cooked through and golden on top, 30 to 35 minutes, rotating both the oven and the lid after 15 minutes to prevent hot spots. Serve warm, of course.

Green Chile and Cheese Cast-iron Cornbread

For a gentler version of this punchy, cheesy cowpoke staple, ditch the poblano for fresh corn kernels from three ears of corn. **Serves 6**

1¼ cups all-purpose flour
1¼ cups fine cornmeal, such as Bob's Red Mill Fine-Ground
¼ cup sugar
2 teaspoons baking powder
¼ teaspoon baking soda
¾ teaspoon kosher salt
1 poblano pepper
1 cup buttermilk
2 large eggs
½ cup (1 stick) unsalted butter, melted and cooled
4 ounces cheddar cheese, shredded (1½ cups)

In the Backpack

- ☐ 10-inch cast-iron Dutch oven
- ☐ Whisk
- ☐ Large liquid measuring cup
- ☐ Mixing bowl

At Home

1. Combine the flour, cornmeal, sugar, baking powder, baking soda, and salt in a gallon-size resealable plastic bag.

2. Char the poblano pepper over an open burner or under the broiler until blackened. Place in a bowl and cover with plastic wrap for 15 minutes. Peel, seed, and mince the pepper. Pack in a resealable plastic container.

At the Campout

3. Prepare a campfire (see page 24) and preheat a 10-inch cast-iron Dutch oven to 375°F (7 hot coals under the oven, 16 on the lid) for 10 minutes.

4. Meanwhile, whisk together the buttermilk, eggs, and melted butter in a large liquid measuring cup. Dump the flour mixture into a medium bowl and make a well in the center. Pour the buttermilk mixture into the well and stir until just combined. Stir in the cheese and minced pepper.

5. Carefully remove the hot Dutch oven from the coals, add the batter, smooth the top, and replace the lid. Bake at 375°F (7 hot coals under the oven, 16 on the lid) for 30 to 35 minutes, rotating both the oven and the lid after 15 minutes to prevent hot spots. The cornbread is finished when the edges begin pulling away from the sides of the Dutch oven and the center springs back when you touch it. If the center needs more time, remove the Dutch oven from the campfire and let it rest with the lid on for an additional 10 minutes. Slice and serve warm.

Grilled Little Gems with Cherry Tomatoes, Nectarines, and Creamy Dill Dressing

We grill these tender, crunchy, irresistible mini romaines on the campfire, then smother them in dilly dressing, as one should. If you can't find Little Gems, use romaine hearts; they're a fine substitute, if somewhat less endearing. If dill's eluding you but your windowsill herb garden's basil plant is out of control, swap the two to make a summery buttermilk basil ranch. **Serves 4**

Creamy Dill Dressing
½ cup buttermilk
¼ cup mayonnaise, preferably Best Foods or Hellmann's
1 tablespoon Dijon mustard
1 tablespoon fresh lemon juice
2 garlic cloves
¼ cup chopped fresh dill (see headnote)
3 green onions, coarsely chopped
½ teaspoon kosher salt
¼ teaspoon freshly ground pepper

Salad
½ pint cherry tomatoes
2 ears of corn
1 large nectarine
6 heads Little Gem lettuce
Olive oil
Fine sea salt and freshly ground pepper

In the Backpack
☐ 12-inch cast-iron skillet
☐ Barbecue tongs
☐ Cutting board
☐ Silicone brush
☐ Serving platter
☐ Salad tongs

At Home

1. To make the dressing: In a food processor, combine the buttermilk, mayonnaise, mustard, lemon juice, garlic, dill, green onions, salt, and pepper and pulse until the dressing is smooth. Transfer to a tall 8-ounce Mason jar and refrigerate.

At the Campout

2. Prepare a campfire (see page 24) and fit it with a grill grate. Remove the dressing from the cooler and let it come to room temperature.

3. To make the salad: Once the flames die down, heat a 12-inch cast-iron skillet on the grate until hot but not smoking and roast the cherry tomatoes until blistered, about 3 minutes. Remove the tomatoes from the heat and grill the corn directly on the campfire grate, then cut the kernels from the cobs. Halve the nectarine and lightly grill it cut-side down on the campfire grate, then cut each half into 8 slices (for 16 slices total).

4. Cut the lettuces in half lengthwise. Brush the cut sides with olive oil and sprinkle with salt and pepper. Grill on the campfire grate until soft and slightly singed, about 3 minutes per side. Plate the lettuce halves on a platter and drizzle with the dressing (give it a good shake first). Sprinkle the corn, tomatoes, and nectarine slices evenly over the top and serve with extra dressing on the side.

Fearsome Foliage: A Forager's Guide to Pernicious Plants

From fiddleheads to edible flowers (hello, wild pansies), the woods are full of friendly fare. But naturalists, be warned: the following flora foes can sneak up on you.

Poison Oak
Toxicodendron diversilobum
The rash from this West Coast menace arrives twelve hours after exposure, which makes for some frenzied retrospective detective work. To muddle the investigation, the leaves could have been red, green, or even red *and* green on the same plant.

Poison Ivy
Toxicodendron radicans
Calamine, cortisone, Benadryl, oatmeal baths, ice cubes, and mittens remain the first line of defense for treating a rash from that nationwide menace, poison ivy. Ignored, symptoms should go away in fourteen days.

Poison Sumac
Toxicodendron vernix
This scarlet-stemmed East Coast sorcerer thrives in the wetlands. As with poison oak and poison ivy, the rash itself is not contagious, but the allergen that causes it, urushiol, lingers on whatever it touches, so be sure to wash clothes, sleeping bags, and towels if contact is suspected.

Stinging Nettle
Urtica dioica
Should you smart from this spade-shaped spectacle, wash the affected area, pacify with the spores of a neighboring fern, and exact revenge by swallowing the pain. Pluck the nettle's tender top leaves, blanch 'em to tame 'em, and swap 'em for spinach.

Jack-O'-Lantern Mushroom
Omphalotus illudens
This orange-hued beauty resembles our favorite fungi, but "false chanterelles" will make you rub your tummy for the wrong reasons. The giveaway is the gills, which are straight and fittingly knife-like rather than forked and melty. Avoid!

Rhubarb
Rheum rhabarbarum
Given all the pleasure and pies derived from this plant's ruby-hued stalks, it's hard to believe its leaves could kill you. And yet.

Four-Leaf Clover
Trifolium
The only danger here is of the green-eyed variety. Only one in ten thousand clovers has four leaves, so finding the luckiest plant in the patch is justifiable grounds for gloating.

Camping Attire

The meals are prepped, the gear is packed, and now it's time to tend to sartorial matters.

Scout's Honor
Whether literally (think *Moonrise Kingdom*, *The Parent Trap*) or figuratively (think *Meatballs*, *Wet Hot American Summer*), a uniform is the tent pole of wilderness outfitting, which loves repetition, subtle variation, and, well, campiness. Our uniform = sun hat + tank + flannel + cutoffs + hiking boots + the occasional bandana, because where else?

Something Wick-ed This Way Comes
Prepare for worse weather by heeding this old adage from frostbitten campers of yore: fleece is your friend, cotton your foe; never leave home without a poncho.

Seven-Layer Trip
When hiking could lead to bouldering could lead to spelunking could lead to cave-diving could lead to basking in the sun could lead to frolicking in the fields could lead to picnicking on a mountaintop could lead to canoodling by the campfire, never has your love of layering been more relevant.

Clever Clogs
Pack podiatry's good cop *and* bad cop: sturdy, sensible, broken-in hiking boots for the trails, and squishy, comfortable slip-ons for the campground.

Lotsa Socks
You'll be the savior of your campout when you reveal the sacred pair of dry socks you squirreled away in that clandestine zipper compartment.

Woolly and Mammoth
Are our criteria for campfire sweaters.

Tip-Top Shape
The Lazarus of camp coiffure, hats revive bug bivvy bedhead in a snap. (To wit: Meryl Streep in *Out of Africa*, John Belushi in *Continental Divide*.) Bring a baseball cap for day and a warm hat for night.

Pride Goeth Before a Fall
Stylish, it is not. But when it's 2:00 A.M. and you've gotta find the primitive potty, your headlamp might be the only thing that keeps your tail out of the poison ivy.

Garden-Raid Tomato, Cucumber, and Melon Salad

Perhaps the one downside of late-summer camping excursions is leaving behind the lush, fruit-laden tomato, cucumber, and melon vines in your home garden. Right before you hit the road, harvest a big boxful, both to make this "garden raid" salad and to share with your neighboring campers, perhaps in exchange for a few of their S'moreos (page 138), because *balance*. Serves 4

Presto Pesto (page 100)
4 medium heirloom
    tomatoes, various colors
2 lemon cucumbers
1 cucumber
½ pint cherry tomatoes,
    various colors
½ small cantaloupe,
    preferably Charentais
1 small shallot
One 8-ounce ball fresh
    mozzarella
¼ cup fresh basil leaves

In the Backpack

☐ Cutting board
☐ Serving platter
☐ Salad tongs

At Home
1. Prepare the Presto Pesto, and reserve half for the salad and half for another use.

At the Campout
2. Remove the pesto from the cooler and let it come to room temperature. Slice the heirloom tomatoes and both types of cucumbers into ¼-inch-thick rounds; cut the cherry tomatoes in half. Arrange the tomatoes and cucumbers in layers on a large platter. Peel and slice the cantaloupe into ½-inch-wide wedges and add to the platter. Slice the shallot into very thin rings and tear the ball of mozzarella into 12 pieces. Sprinkle the salad with the shallot rings and basil leaves, and dot with the mozzarella pieces. Drizzle with Presto Pesto and serve.

Red Cabbage, Jicama, and Orange Slaw

Sturdy and simple, with a zesty south-of-the-border bent, this beautiful slaw will bring a blast of color and flavor to the campout table. Tossing the cabbage with salt and giving it a time-out will tenderize it; if it releases quite a lot of water, give it a paper towel pat-down before adding the rest of the ingredients. **Serves 4**

Lime-Cumin Vinaigrette
1 teaspoon grated lime zest
2 tablespoons fresh lime juice
1 tablespoon honey
1 teaspoon ground cumin
¼ teaspoon kosher salt
2 tablespoons extra-virgin olive oil
2 tablespoons grapeseed oil

Slaw
4 cups finely shredded red cabbage (from about ½ large cabbage)
1 teaspoon kosher salt
½ jicama bulb, julienned
6 radishes, thinly sliced
2 oranges, peeled, trimmed, sliced into ¼-inch-thick rounds, and seeded
1 cup fresh cilantro leaves, very coarsely chopped
2 green onions, thinly sliced on an angle
2 tablespoons hulled roasted salted sunflower seeds

1 Fresno chile, thinly sliced on an angle, for garnish
2 tablespoons hulled roasted sunflower seeds, for garnish

In the Backpack
☐ Large mixing bowl
☐ Serving bowl or platter
☐ Salad tongs

At Home
1. To make the vinaigrette: Whisk together the lime zest, lime juice, honey, cumin, and salt in a small bowl, then add the olive oil and the grapeseed oil in a thin stream, whisking until emulsified. Transfer the vinaigrette to a 4-ounce Mason jar and refrigerate.

At the Campout
2. Remove the vinaigrette from the cooler and bring to room temperature.

3. To make the slaw: In a large mixing bowl, toss the cabbage with the salt and set aside for 15 minutes. Add the jicama, radishes, oranges, cilantro, green onions, and sunflower seeds. Give the vinaigrette a good shake. Drizzle the slaw with vinaigrette and gently mix.

4. Transfer to a serving bowl or platter and garnish with the chile slices and sunflower seeds.

MENU

Buckaroo Banquet

Fit for flinty-eyed cowboys and famished city folk alike, this hearty spread will put meat on your bones and bourbon in your belly.

Forest Fondue 67

Grilled Little Gems with Cherry Tomatoes, Nectarines, and Creamy Dill Dressing 79

Sautéed Chanterelle Mushrooms 69

Hasselbackpack Potatoes 72

Green Chile and Cheese Cast-iron Cornbread 78

Big Sky Rib-Eye with Shallot-Herb Butter 132

Molten Chocolate Orange Campfire Cakes 155

Off-the-Grid Old-Fashioneds 160

Fire-Roasted Vegetables with Black Lentils

Cooked lentils keep for several days in the refrigerator, so you can reduce your campout efforts by preparing the black lentils at home (as instructed in step 3), then transporting them to the campsite in the cooler. If they seem stiff and unsociable, warm them up in a skillet before letting them loose to mix and mingle with the grilled vegetables. **Serves 4**

Kalamata-Anchovy Dressing
2 tablespoons red wine vinegar
2 teaspoons Dijon mustard
1 teaspoon anchovy paste
1 garlic clove, minced
¼ cup finely chopped pitted kalamata olives
⅛ teaspoon freshly ground pepper
½ cup extra-virgin olive oil

Salad
1½ cups black lentils
4 cups vegetable or chicken stock
1 teaspoon kosher salt, plus more as needed
2 sprigs fresh thyme
2 garlic cloves, smashed
1 small bulb fennel, trimmed and cut into 8 wedges, fronds reserved
1 small head Romanesco, divided into large florets (see Tiny Tip)
1 medium eggplant, sliced into ¼-inch-thick rounds
2 red bell peppers, halved and seeded
Extra-virgin olive oil
Freshly ground pepper
1 bunch green onions

At Home
1. To make the dressing: Whisk together the vinegar, mustard, anchovy paste, garlic, olives, and black pepper in a small bowl. Add the olive oil in a thin stream, continuing to whisk until emulsified. Transfer the dressing to an 8-ounce Mason jar and refrigerate.

At the Campout
2. Prepare a campfire (see page 24) and fit it with a grill grate. Set up the camp stove. Remove the dressing from the cooler and let it come to room temperature.

3. To make the salad: Combine the lentils, stock, salt, thyme, and garlic in a large saucepan. Bring to a boil over medium-high heat on the camp stove, then reduce the heat to maintain a simmer and cook until the lentils are tender, about 30 minutes. Drain the lentils and transfer to a large mixing bowl.

4. Place the fennel, Romanesco, eggplant, and bell peppers on a large rimmed baking sheet, brush with olive oil, and sprinkle with salt and black pepper. Grill the vegetables over the campfire, turning occasionally so that they cook evenly. As the vegetables soften and begin to char, pull them off the grill and transfer to the bowl with the lentils (except for the red peppers— place them in a paper bag to sweat, then peel and tear them into 1-inch-long strips before adding to the bowl). Grill the green onions last, as they cook very quickly, and set aside for garnish.

In the Backpack

☐ Large saucepan

☐ Large mixing bowl

☐ Large rimmed baking sheet

☐ Barbecue tongs

☐ Paper bag

☐ Serving platter

☐ Salad tongs

5. Drizzle the lentils and vegetables with the dressing (give it a good shake first) and gently toss. Arrange the salad on a platter, top with the whole grilled green onions and reserved fennel fronds, and serve.

***

tiny tip: We love to use Romanesco in this salad because it's both delicious and unusually beautiful, but cauliflower will do the trick, as will broccoli rabe.

Wheat Berries, Plums, and Golden Beets with Walnut Oil Vinaigrette

A grain salad is a natural fit for camping, since it's a meal unto itself that stands the test of time and invites improvisation. You can make the base of this salad several days ahead, riff on this recipe with your favorite grain of the moment—we see you, amaranth—and swap in any leftover stone fruit or apples lingering in your backpack. The key ingredient is roasted walnut oil, such as La Tourangelle's. Its toasty flavor is a salad game-changer. **Serves 4 to 6**

Walnut Oil Vinaigrette
2 tablespoons cider vinegar
1 teaspoon Dijon mustard
1 teaspoon honey
½ teaspoon fresh thyme
    leaves
¼ teaspoon kosher salt
⅛ teaspoon freshly ground
    pepper
½ cup roasted walnut oil

Salad
2 large golden beets
¾ cup walnuts
1 cup wheat berries
1 teaspoon kosher salt
4 stalks celery
2 ounces feta cheese,
    crumbled
1 plum
½ pint blackberries

In the Backpack
☐ Serving bowl
☐ Salad tongs

At Home

1. To make the vinaigrette: Whisk together the vinegar, mustard, honey, thyme, salt, and pepper in a small bowl. Add the walnut oil in a thin stream, continuing to whisk until emulsified. Set aside.

2. Preheat the oven to 400°F. Line a baking sheet with parchment paper.

3. To make the salad: Scrub the beets, trim their tops and tails, wrap them in foil, and roast until tender, 45 minutes to 1 hour. Once they're cool, peel and cut into ½-inch cubes to yield about 1½ cups.

4. Reduce the oven temperature to 350°F. Toast the walnuts on the prepared baking sheet until fragrant and one shade darker, about 8 minutes. Once they're cool, roughly chop.

Variation

To finish the salad at home rather than on-site, omit the celery leaves (which will wilt) and swap ½ cup dried black currants for the fresh fruit. Plump the currants by covering them with boiling water for 10 minutes and draining before adding to the salad.

5. Bring the wheat berries, 1 quart water, and the salt to a boil in a medium saucepan over high heat. Reduce the heat to maintain a simmer and cook until tender, 45 minutes to 1 hour. Drain. Pour onto a sheet pan and blot with a paper towel.

6. Transfer the warm wheat berries to a large resealable container, mix with half the dressing, and let cool. Thinly slice the celery on an angle and reserve the tender leaves. Add the sliced celery, walnuts, and feta to the wheat berries and toss to combine. Pack the remaining dressing, ¼ cup (lightly packed) of the reserved celery leaves, and the fruit in a cooler filled with ice.

At the Campout

7. Remove the vinaigrette from the cooler and let it come to room temperature. Give it a good shake.

8. Transfer the wheat berries to a serving bowl and refresh with more dressing if needed. Slice the plum into thin wedges and add to the salad with the blackberries and celery leaves. Drizzle with a little dressing, and gently toss. Taste and add more dressing if needed before serving.

Summer Squash, Snap Pea, and Asparagus Salad

Taste the summer rainbow in this brightly colored *and* flavored salad, which is an excellent way to make a dent in your CSA box. When choosing asparagus, look for the thinnest spears; they're particularly crisp and snappy eaten raw. Should you forget to pack the vegetable peeler, use your cheese slicer or handheld mandoline. Should you forget to pack those (for shame!), slice the zucchini into paper-thin rounds instead of ribbons; they won't be quite as comely, but they'll get the job done. **Serves 4**

Meyer Lemon Vinaigrette

2 tablespoons red wine vinegar
1 tablespoon fresh Meyer lemon juice
1 tablespoon Dijon mustard
¼ teaspoon grated lemon zest
¼ teaspoon kosher salt
⅛ teaspoon freshly ground pepper
½ cup canola oil

Salad

2 green zucchini
2 yellow squash
½ pound thin asparagus spears
1 cup snap peas
2 large rainbow carrots
½ cup fresh mint leaves, finely chopped
12 fresh chives, minced

2 ounces ricotta salata cheese, crumbled, for garnish
¼ cup coarsely chopped roasted almonds, for garnish

At Home

1. To make the vinaigrette: Whisk together the vinegar, lemon juice, Dijon, lemon zest, salt, and pepper in a small bowl, then add the canola oil in a thin stream, whisking constantly to emulsify. Pour the vinaigrette into a tall 8-ounce Mason jar and refrigerate.

At the Campout

2. Remove the vinaigrette from the cooler and let it come to room temperature.

3. To make the salad: Using a vegetable peeler or handheld mandoline, slice the zucchini and yellow squash lengthwise into thin ribbons. Trim the woody ends off the asparagus and cut or snap each spear into 2-inch lengths. (If your asparagus is on the thicker side, shave it lengthwise, à la the zucchini.) Slice the snap peas in half on the bias and slice the carrots into ⅛-inch-thick rounds.

In the Backpack

- ☐ Vegetable peeler or handheld mandoline (see Tiny Tip)
- ☐ Large mixing bowl
- ☐ Serving platter
- ☐ Salad tongs

4. In a large mixing bowl, combine the zucchini, yellow squash, asparagus, snap peas, carrots, mint, and chives, drizzle with the vinaigrette (give it a good shake first), and gently toss to mix. Arrange the salad on a serving platter and sprinkle with the ricotta salata and almonds.

tiny tip: Even when camping, you'll find plenty of uses for a handheld Japanese mandoline, from shaving zucchini ribbons to slicing breakfast potatoes. A good-quality version can be had for less than twenty dollars; buy one and keep it with the camp kitchen supplies.

Chapter 4

Campfire Mains

The sun's bid adieu for the day, the first round of flask cocktails is but a fond memory, and the coals are glowing invitingly, signaling the start of a spectacular stick-to-your-ribs supper that will live forever in campout lore. Nimbly assemble a savory Tinfoil Shrimp Boil, pass around piping-hot bowls of Backcountry Beef Stew, or conspire with your trusty cast-iron skillet to dish up Skillet-Fried Rainbow Trout with Lemon and Fresh Dill. By the time the crickets commence their twilight serenade, your fellow fire-goers will be wholly impressed with the impeccable campfire cooking skills they never knew you had.

Sliced Tri-Tip Sandwich Bar

Light the fire upon arrival, and by the time the tents are staked, you'll be ready for a steak lunch that sets the buffet bar high for the rest of the trip. Thanks to a couple of swift home kitchen projects and a brief stop at the bakery, all that's left to do at the campout is toss the roast on the grill, lean back in your camp chair, and await the *ooh*s and *aah*s. **Makes 6 sandwiches**

1 whole beef tri-tip
   (about 2 pounds)
Sage-Coffee Rub
   (see page 126)
Quickled Red Onions
   (recipe follows)
Horseradish Crème Fraîche
   (recipe follows)
6 demi-baguettes, sliced
   open
2 bunches watercress
4 ounces blue cheese,
   crumbled

In the Backpack

- ☐ Barbecue tongs
- ☐ Meat thermometer
- ☐ Steak knife
- ☐ Platter

At Home

1. Massage the tri-tip with an entire jar of Sage-Coffee Rub and place it in a gallon-size resealable plastic bag.

2. Make the Quickled Red Onions and Horseradish Crème Fraîche.

At the Campout

3. Bring the tri-tip to room temperature. Prepare a campfire (see page 24) and fit it with a grill grate. Grade the coals under the grill so they are thicker/hotter on one side.

4. Sear the tri-tip on the hottest part of the grill for 5 minutes per side. Move the tri-tip to medium heat and grill until medium-rare, an additional 10 minutes per pound, or until the internal temperature reaches 130°F. Rest for 10 minutes.

5. Slice the steak thinly against the grain and place on a platter. Set out all the goods in a beguiling buffet and invite the campers to make sandwiches. For the works: Spread the horseradish cream on a baguette and pile high with the steak, watercress, pickled onions, and a sprinkle of blue cheese.

Quickled Red Onions

Makes one 1 pint jar

1 red onion, thinly sliced into rings
5 black peppercorns
5 allspice berries
1 bay leaf

1 cup white wine vinegar
1 teaspoon sugar
1 teaspoon kosher salt

Fill a 1-pint Mason jar with the sliced red onion, peppercorns, allspice berries, and bay leaf. Combine the vinegar, sugar, and salt in a medium saucepan and bring to a boil over medium heat, stirring until the sugar and salt dissolve. Remove and discard the bay leaf. Pour into the jar. Cool completely, cover, and refrigerate.

Horseradish Crème Fraîche

Makes one 8-ounce jar

1 cup crème fraîche
½ cup grated fresh horseradish root
  (find it near the gingerroot)
1 tablespoon finely chopped
  fresh chives

1 teaspoon Dijon mustard
1 teaspoon fresh
  lemon juice
½ teaspoon kosher salt

Whisk all the ingredients together in a small bowl, transfer to an 8-ounce Mason jar, and refrigerate.

12 Toasty Pudgie Pies

As if saying "pudgie pies" weren't fun enough, you get to actually *make* them, in one of the most ingenious of camping gadgets, the pie iron, which is essentially two long-handled mini cast-iron skillets clasped together. The rules of pie iron engagement are simple—butter a slice of bread, place it buttered-side down on one half of the iron, build your sandwich on top, cover with the second slice of bread (buttered-side up), squeeze the pie iron shut, and hold it over the coals until your pudgie pie is nice and toasty, 3 to 5 minutes per side.

Since you'll need to keep the cooking time brisk to avoid burning everything to a crisp, be sure to work with fully cooked meats, and for savory sandwiches, slather mayonnaise on the outside in lieu of butter for an even richer effect. For a merry, melty family meal, set out a build-your-own pudgie pie bar, and let the creative clasping begin. Start with these suggestions, and then feel free to go off the grid and get inventive!

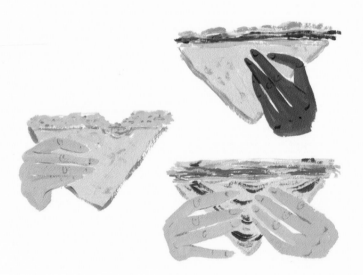

1. Pimento cheese + heirloom tomato + sourdough bread

2. Raspberry jam + Cinnamon Sunbutter (page 48) + whole wheat bread

3. Pears + Gorgonzola Dolce + brioche

4. Honeycrisp apple + almond butter + cinnamon swirl bread

5. Pastrami + Swiss + sauerkraut + Thousand Island dressing + marbled rye bread

6. Mortadella + soppressata + capicola + provolone + pickled peppers + ciabatta

7. Prosciutto + Taleggio + onion jam + fresh figs + focaccia

8. Ham + scrambled egg + Fontina + English muffin

9. Leftover Dutch Oven Roast Chicken (page 114) + green chiles + Monterey Jack + whole wheat pita

10. Roast beef + sautéed peppers and onions + American cheese + white bread

11. Hamburger patty (cooked) + Swiss + sautéed onion + rye bread

12. Breakfast sausage links (cooked) + cheddar + maple syrup + freezer waffles

Chorizo Skillet Nachos

Soggy chips are nachos' greatest nemesis, so when perusing the snack aisle, choose a chip with stamina—because supporting a pyramid of spicy ground chorizo, melty Monterey Jack cheese, fresh homemade pico de gallo, and other finger-lickin' fixins is hard work. **Serves 4**

½ pound ground (fresh) chorizo
Pico de Gallo (page 201)
10 ounces Monterey Jack cheese, grated
One 14-ounce bag corn tortilla chips
1 avocado, diced
Sour cream
Fresh cilantro leaves

___

In the Backpack

☐ 12-inch cast-iron skillet
☐ Foil

At Home

1. Brown the chorizo in a skillet over medium heat and let cool. Prepare the pico de gallo. Pack the chorizo, pico de gallo, and cheese in separate resealable containers and refrigerate.

At the Campout

2. Prepare a campfire (see page 24).

3. Cherry-pick your finest chip specimens (saving the broken bits for Pedal-to-the-Metal Migas, page 200) and carefully construct three layers of chips, cheese, and chorizo in a 12-inch cast-iron skillet. Cover the skillet tightly with foil and place directly in the campfire coals until the chips are crisped and the cheese is melted, 8 to 10 minutes. Remove the nachos from the coals, uncover, and garnish with pico de gallo, avocado, sour cream, and cilantro. Dig in and wash down with a cold beer.

Skillet Pizza Primer

With proper preparation and a cast-iron skillet or two, taking pizza night outside is a cool mountain breeze. Here are the basic principles of alfresco pizza making, from setting up your prep station to preventing singed dough *and* digits.

Rolling in the Dough

When prepping Perfect Pizza Dough (page 101), plan on at least one 12-inch pizza per person (two for Big Sky–size appetites), and bring a few extra dough balls, too—you can use them for hot Roasted Garlic Parmesan Monkey Bread (page 77), dinner rolls, flatbread, and bacon 'n' egg breakfast pizzas.

SOS (Set Out Snacks)

Making skillet pizza isn't for the impatient—if you're working with a standard-issue campground fire pit, you're likely baking only one or two at a time, so feeding the whole crew is a relaxed process (to enjoy pies in their prime, it's best to slice them immediately and eat them hot off the fire, versus stockpiling them until they're all cooked). Make it fun by cranking up the pizza playlist and putting out plenty of trail snacks and ice-cold grapefruit radlers.

The Tao of Toppings

Once your round of dough hits the hot skillet, you'll need to work quickly, so have cheese grated, toppings sliced and diced, and your *mise en place* within easy reach of the fire pit (a small folding table or large rimmed baking sheet set over a sturdy stump works well). To easily organize all your accoutrements, bring a stack of lightweight 1-pint deli containers.

Turn Up the Heat

One of the best ways to sustain steady and powerful heat beneath your pizza is to stick your cast-iron skillet straight onto the hot coals, versus on the grill grate. Once the fire has ebbed, leaving red-hot coals dusted with gray ash, spread the coals thickly and evenly in the fire pit, then let the skillet heat until very hot but not smoking, about 10 minutes, before wiping out any stray ash, patting the dough into a circle (or having the hotsy-totsy camp chef on the next page do it for you), placing the dough inside, and adding toppings. Rotate the skillet midway through cooking to ensure even baking. When the pizza is cooked through, the dough will be gorgeously browned and crispy on the bottom but pale on top—worry not, it's just as delicious. That said, to impart a golden glow to the top of your dough, heat the lid of a 12-inch cast-iron Dutch oven in the coals, and place it over the skillet while your pizza's cooking.

Fireproof Your Fingers

Cast-iron burns mean business, so wear heatproof mitts that cover your wrists when handling hot skillets, use a long-handled spoon to spread sauce on the dough, and apply toppings with utmost care. Should things get a little too heated despite your best efforts, keep ice, burn salve, and Band-Aids at the ready.

Rucksack Red Sauce

As camping season approaches, prep this easy red sauce and freeze it so it's cooler-ready. When summer herbs are at their peak, we like to stir a handful of chopped fresh basil into the finished batch. **Makes about 1 quart**

¼ cup extra-virgin olive oil
3 large garlic cloves, minced
One 28-ounce can San Marzano puréed tomatoes
½ teaspoon kosher salt
¼ teaspoon freshly ground pepper

Heat the olive oil in a medium saucepan over medium-low heat, add the garlic, and cook until the garlic is fragrant and lightly toasted, about 1 minute. Add the tomatoes, salt, and pepper. Bring to a boil, reduce the heat to maintain a simmer, and cook for 1 hour. Let cool, transfer to a 1-quart Mason jar, and refrigerate.

Presto Pesto

If making this summery spread ahead of time, portion it into 4-ounce jelly jars, top each with a splash of olive oil to prevent the pesto from oxidizing, and freeze for future uses great and small. **Makes about 2 cups**

3 cups packed fresh basil leaves
3 large garlic cloves
1 cup coarsely grated Parmesan, preferably Parmigiano-Reggiano
⅓ cup pine nuts
¾ cup extra-virgin olive oil, plus more for the jar
1½ teaspoons kosher salt
¾ teaspoon freshly ground pepper

Purée the basil, garlic, Parmesan, pine nuts, olive oil, salt, and pepper in a food processor until smooth. Transfer to a 1-pint Mason jar, top with a thin layer of olive oil, and refrigerate.

Perfect Pizza Dough

This is the only dough you'll ever need in the wild, be it for skillet pizzas or Roasted Garlic Parmesan Monkey Bread (page 77), or to wind around a forked stick and bake over the fire for bread (on) sticks. This dough's a real handful, so use a large food processor to make the full recipe.
Makes four 12-inch pizzas

2 cups warm water (110° to 115°F)
3 tablespoons extra-virgin olive oil
1 tablespoon honey
4½ cups bread flour, plus more for dusting
One ¼-ounce packet active dry yeast (about 2¼ teaspoons)
2 teaspoons kosher salt

In the Backpack

☐ Large cutting board
☐ Metal barbecue spatula

At Home

1. Whisk together the warm water, olive oil, and honey in a small bowl.

2. Pulse the bread flour, yeast, and salt in a food processor until combined, about 5 seconds. Add the wet ingredients and process until a dough ball forms, 15 to 20 seconds. Let the dough process for 10 to 15 seconds more. The dough will be wet and sticky, with a slight stretch to it.

3. With floured hands, remove the dough from the processor and place it on a floured surface. Knead for a few seconds, then divide the dough into 4 equal portions. Tuck the edges under to form a ball and place each ball in a 1-quart resealable container or gallon-size resealable plastic bag. Refrigerate the dough for at least 24 hours and up to 3 days. Transport it to the campsite in a cooler, along with a small container of flour.

At the Campout

4. Remove the dough from the cooler. With floured hands, remove each portion of dough from its container or bag, place it on a floured surface, and tuck the edges under again to re-form a ball. Let the dough balls rest at room temperature for 1 hour before cooking. Follow the recipe on page 102 to finish your pizza.

Wood-Fired Skillet Pizzas

Pack the cooler with dough (see page 101) and toppings, and take your *pizzaiolo* skills to places they've never been—literally. Each recipe makes one 12-inch skillet pizza, so you can mix and match, or multiply. Pizzas take about 10 minutes to cook over hot coals; when they're done baking, use a long-handled metal barbecue spatula to carefully transfer the pie to a cutting board, then toss the next round in and keep going.

Fennel Sausage, Calabrian Chile, Onion, and Olives

¼ cup Rucksack Red Sauce (page 100)
¼ pound ground Italian sausage, cooked
½ cup shredded whole-milk mozzarella cheese

⅛ red onion, sliced paper-thin
¼ cup Castelvetrano olives, pitted and torn in half
1 Calabrian chile, thinly sliced

Prosciutto, Figs, Basil, Black Pepper, and Honey

2 tablespoons extra-virgin olive oil
¼ cup shredded whole-milk mozzarella cheese
1 ounce thinly sliced prosciutto

2 fresh figs, cut into 6 wedges
¼ cup fresh basil leaves
Pinch of freshly cracked black pepper
Drizzle of honey, to finish

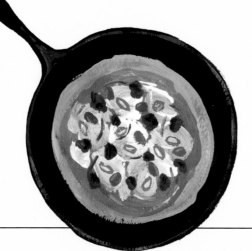

Leek, Lemon, Shiitake, and Thyme

¼ cup Rucksack Red Sauce (page 100)
½ cup shredded whole-milk
  mozzarella cheese
1 leek, halved lengthwise, grilled, and
  thinly sliced

1 small lemon, sliced paper-thin
3 shiitake mushrooms, sliced
  paper-thin
Sprinkling of fresh thyme leaves

Squash Blossoms, Cherry Tomatoes, and Presto Pesto

¼ cup Presto Pesto (page 100)
One 4-ounce ball fresh
  mozzarella cheese, sliced into
  ¼-inch-thick rounds

4 squash blossoms
½ pint cherry tomatoes, blistered
  in a hot skillet

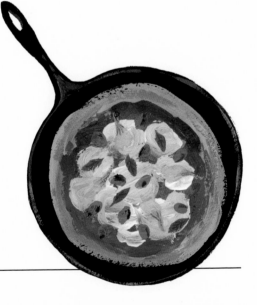

Camping in Your Own Backyard

Not quite ready to venture far from home? Simply step out the back door. The wild awaits, if you use your imagination. Here's how to get started.

- Collect phones. Turn off Wi-Fi. You're going off the grid.

- Set up the fire pit, pitch a tent/ procure a yurt, and suspend your disbelief that the garden is now a campground, with one exception: the house bathroom can be used, but only by flashlight.

- And speaking of flashlights, tonight is the night for an all-neighborhood game of flashlight tag, kick the can, tug-of-war, or Twister.

- To maximize ambiance, plan a menu that requires fire-cooking. Unfurl the aluminum and set out the fixings for foil packets (see page 73), ready the cast-iron troops for skillet pizzas (see page 102), or hang a Dutch oven of chili (see page 108) on a tripod over the campfire.

- When supper ends, start the ghost stories. Extra points for involving creepy neighbors, rabid raccoons, possessed tree houses, or recent spectral sightings. Pro tip: The sudden introduction of a rubber tarantula can be very effective.

- Kick off the s'mores bar: Pile homemade marshmallows on a pedestal, arrange an array of chocolates and cookies (see page 138) on baking sheets, ready the roasting sticks, and issue each camper a personal packet of Wet-Naps.

- Neighborhood association be damned—it's time for a drum circle.

- Tuck in, or quietly tiptoe back to the comfort of your own bed. If your transgression hasn't been discovered by morning (if it was, you likely got a swirly), reappear with pancakes and all will be forgiven.

MENU

Plein Air Pizza Night

Stoke the campfire, pour a cold pale ale, and make pizza night an open-air affair.

Beerlao Nut Chow 52

Furikake Flurry 53

Wood-Fired Skillet Pizzas 102

Ember-Baked Apricots with Honey and Rosemary 74

Chocolate Chunk Cowboy Cookie 151
and vanilla bean ice cream sandwiches

Pale ale and pilsner

Five-Point-Buck Jelly Shots 177

Catchall Carnitas

Nothing is more welcome in the woods than a multiuse item. And if a Pocket Monkey has a culinary corollary, it's carnitas. Pulled pork shoulder is delicious for days, with limitless applications, from skillet pizzas (page 102) to nachos (page 98) to breakfast burritos (page 198). For a taco night, hit the resupply station for all the goods detailed at right. **Serves 4**

1 tablespoon kosher salt
2 teaspoons freshly ground pepper
1 tablespoon ground ancho chile
1 tablespoon dried Mexican oregano
2 teaspoons onion powder
3 pounds pork shoulder, cut into 3-inch chunks
2 teaspoons cumin seeds
1 cinnamon stick
1 white onion
4 garlic cloves
2 bay leaves
2 oranges
1 lime
2 cups chicken stock
2 tablespoons vegetable oil

In the Backpack

☐ Two 12-inch cast-iron skillets
☐ Serving spoon

At Home

1. Position a rack in the center of the oven. Preheat the oven to 325°F.

2. In a large bowl, combine the salt, pepper, ancho chile, oregano, and onion powder, then add the pork shoulder and toss. Heat a 6-quart Dutch oven over medium heat and toast the cumin seeds and cinnamon stick until fragrant. Remove from the heat. Quarter the onion, peel and smash the garlic cloves, and add to the Dutch oven with the bay leaves. Juice the oranges and lime, discard the seeds, and add the juice and rinds to the pot. Add the pork, arrange the mixture in an even layer, and pour in the stock to just cover it. Partially cover and cook until very tender, about 3 hours.

3. Remove the pork and set it aside in a bowl. Remove the cinnamon stick, bay leaves, onion, and citrus rinds and strain the liquid through a strainer set over a large liquid measuring cup. Using two forks, shred the pork. Pour the cooking liquid over the pork and pack in a plastic container with a trustworthy lid.

At the Campout

4. Prepare a campfire (see page 24) and fit it with a grill grate, or set up the camp stove. Heat two 12-inch cast-iron skillets on the campfire grill grate or on the camp stove over high heat until very hot but not smoking, about 10 minutes. Slick the surface of each skillet with a tablespoon of vegetable oil and add the carnitas. Press down with the back of a wooden spoon.

5. Cook the carnitas until heated through and beginning to crisp on one side. To avoid a skirmish over the crispy bits, make sure there are lots; let the pork sit in the skillet for a hot minute before stirring. Assemble into tacos, pile into a baked potato, top a pizza, or stuff a burrito.

Tacos by Twilight

Few meals are as easy or crowd-pleasy as taco night, so while your carnitas cooks, assemble this fuss-free taco bar, then summon everyone to the picnic table with a few shakes of the maracas, and let the tortilla topping begin.

- Wrap fresh corn tortillas in foil, and let them warm near the fire. Plan on three tortillas per camper, but a few extras never hurt—it's a well-known fact that exposure to the great outdoors amplifies appetites.

- For herbivores, sauté a skilletful of seasonal vegetables—squash, potatoes, onions, and mushrooms.

- Pack in canned pinto beans, black beans, or refried beans, and a batch of precooked Mexican rice, and warm them in saucepans on the camp stove or campfire.

- Chop, grate, slice, and dice fundamental fillers like lettuce, cabbage, tomatoes, onion, cheese, and fresh cilantro, and set out alongside salsa (verde and roja, *por favor*), pico de gallo (page 201), sour cream, guacamole, pickled onions, and lime wedges.

- Chill a bucket of Coronas, Dos Equis, or Negra Modelo, pour the *tepache* (page 174), and/or distribute tequila shots. For no-proof imbibers, break out the Jarritos or MexiCoke.

- Turn up Spotify's Taco Tuesdays playlist, and dig in!

Spicy Chuckwagon Chili

Mix up a few batches of chili powder and stock your camp-cooking larder with canned beans, tomatoes, peppers, and tomato paste, and you'll be ready for a season of spectacular camp suppers. (Grab the fresh meat-and-veg en route to the campsite.) Spicy oak-smoked Spanish paprika, aka *pimentón de la Vera picante*, lends a wisp of fire smoke to this versatile classic chile con carne, which can be made with any ground meat you like. **Serves 6**

Chili Powder

1 tablespoon dried oregano
1 tablespoon ground cumin
2 teaspoons ground
    ancho chile
1 teaspoon garlic powder
½ teaspoon ground coriander
2 teaspoons pimentón de
    la Vera picante
¼ teaspoon ground cinnamon
2 teaspoons kosher salt
1 teaspoon freshly
    ground pepper
1 bay leaf

Chili

2 tablespoons extra-virgin
    olive oil
1½ pounds ground beef
1 large onion, chopped
4 garlic cloves, minced
1 red bell pepper, seeded
    and chopped
2 tablespoons tomato paste
One 28-ounce can diced
    tomatoes
One 16-ounce lager-
    style beer
One 15-ounce can pinto
    beans, drained and rinsed
One 15-ounce can kidney
    beans, drained and rinsed
Two 8-ounce cans diced
    green chiles (see Tiny Tip)

In the Backpack

☐ 12-inch cast-iron
    Dutch oven

At Home

1. To make the chili powder: Combine all the chili powder ingredients in an 8-ounce Mason jar labeled "chili powder," because you will later look at this and wonder, and shake to mix.

At the Campout

2. Prepare a campfire (see page 24).

3. To make the chili: Heat the olive oil in a 12-inch cast-iron Dutch oven over medium-high heat. Brown the ground beef and add the onion, garlic, bell pepper, tomato paste, and the whole jar of chili powder. Cook for 5 minutes.

4. Add the tomatoes, beer, beans, and chiles. Bring to a boil, then move the Dutch oven to a cooler area, or ideally a tripod over the campfire, to maintain a simmer and cook for 2 hours. Remove and discard the bay leaf. Ring the dinner bell.

tiny tip: If you're in a pepper-hand safe environment, substitute one large or two small roasted, seeded, and peeled poblano peppers for the canned chiles.

Chili, 5 Ways

Because there's no wrong way to eat it.

1. Cincinnati-Style

4. Come to Papa

2. Frito Pie

3. Chili Dog

5. Tamale Pie

Backcountry Beef Stew

Our rich beef stew has a few technique tips: forgo pre-chopped beef for larger chunks of the optimal cut; deglaze with plenty of booze for a rich, irresistible gravy; add sautéed vegetables halfway through the cooking time to obliterate mush; and (toughest of all) wait a day before eating. Reheat the stew in a Dutch oven hanging from a tripod over the fire. **Serves 6**

3 pounds beef chuck roast, cut into 1½-inch cubes
Kosher salt and freshly ground pepper
Extra-virgin olive oil
12 ounces cremini mushrooms, quartered
3 carrots, halved lengthwise and cut into 2-inch segments
10 ounces pearl onions (preferably red), peeled
1 yellow onion, chopped
8 garlic cloves, minced
¼ cup brandy
1 cup red wine
4 cups beef stock
2 tablespoons Worcestershire sauce
Bouquet garni: 2 bay leaves and 5 sprigs fresh thyme tied into a bundle with kitchen string
2 tablespoons tomato paste
3 tablespoons all-purpose flour
1 pound small yellow potatoes, peeled and halved
½ cup frozen green peas

At Home

1. In a medium bowl, season the beef with 1 tablespoon salt and 2 teaspoons pepper. Refrigerate overnight.

2. Preheat the oven to 325°F.

3. Remove the beef from the refrigerator and pat it dry with paper towels. Heat 2 tablespoons olive oil in a large enameled Dutch oven over medium-high heat. Working in batches, and replacing the olive oil each round, sear the beef until brown, 7 to 10 minutes per batch. Set the beef aside in a bowl.

4. Add the mushrooms to the Dutch oven and cook for 5 minutes. Add the carrots and pearl onions and cook for 10 minutes more. Set the vegetables aside.

5. Add the yellow onion and cook, stirring, until soft, about 8 minutes. Add the garlic and cook for 1 minute. Increase the heat to high, add the brandy and wine, and cook for 3 minutes, scraping the bottom of the pot with a wooden spoon, until the alcohol has reduced by three-quarters. Add the stock, Worcestershire, bouquet garni, and tomato

- ☐ 12-inch cast-iron Dutch oven
- ☐ Ladle

paste. Toss the beef and any juices from the bowl with the flour and add to the stew.

6. Bring the stew to a simmer, partially cover with a lid, and move it to the oven to simmer for 1 hour 15 minutes. Return the vegetables to the stew, add the potatoes, partially cover, and cook for 1 hour more, until the meat is tender and a fork easily pierces a potato. Stir in the peas. Season with salt and pepper. Let cool, and remove and discard the bouquet garni. Skim the fat, if any, then transfer the stew to a resealable container and transport in a cooler filled with ice.

At the Campout
7. Prepare a campfire (see page 24).

8. Reheat the stew in a 12-inch cast-iron Dutch oven over medium heat or swinging from a tripod. Serve piping hot.

Braised Bratwurst and Camp Stove Caraway Cabbage

Simple and satisfying, this fireside supper comes together quickly. If you're camping with only one pot, cook the bratwurst first, set it aside on a plate, and return it to the pot to heat through when the cabbage begins to soften. Serve with whole-grain mustard and crusty bread, or little golden potatoes boiled until fork-tender and tossed with butter, pepper, fresh dill, and flaky salt. **Serves 4 to 6**

Sausage
2 tablespoons extra-virgin olive oil
6 bratwurst sausages

Cabbage
4 ounces thick-cut bacon, sliced into ½-inch pieces
1 large yellow onion, thinly sliced
1 savoy cabbage, cored and thinly sliced
2 teaspoons caraway seeds (see Tiny Tip)
¼ cup red wine vinegar, or more to taste
1 tablespoon dark brown sugar
1 teaspoon kosher salt
½ teaspoon freshly ground pepper

In the Backpack

☐ 12-inch cast-iron skillet
☐ Barbecue tongs
☐ Dutch oven
☐ Serving platter
☐ Serving spoon

1. Set up the camp stove.

2. To cook the sausage: Combine the olive oil and ½ cup water in a 12-inch cast-iron skillet over medium heat. Prick the bratwurst all over with a fork and add to the skillet. Cook for 15 minutes, turning once. Turn up the heat to medium-high and boil off the water. Flip the sausages so they brown on all sides.

3. Meanwhile, make the cabbage: Cook the bacon in a large Dutch oven over medium-high heat until crisp. Transfer to a plate. Add the onion and cook in the bacon grease for 5 minutes. Add the cabbage and caraway seeds and cook until the cabbage has wilted, about 7 minutes. Add the vinegar, brown sugar, salt, and pepper and cook for 10 minutes more, until the cabbage is soft. Return the bacon to the dish. Taste, add another tablespoon of vinegar if the cabbage needs a little more zip, and adjust the seasoning.

4. Transfer the cabbage to a serving platter and top with the brats.

tiny tip: For extra camp-cooking points, toast the caraway seeds in a small skillet over medium heat until fragrant, then bruise them with a nearby (clean) rock or with that mortar and pestle you just couldn't leave behind.

Gimme Shelter: Creating a Comfortable Campsite

If you've ever dreamed of arriving at the campground to find the site magically pre-set (by gnomes perhaps?), so all you have to do is be greeted by design perfection and a camping butler, then you'll understand why Kelsey and Mike Sheofsky's high-end outdoor events company, Shelter Co., is in demand. Here Kelsey shares her secrets to designing an artful home so very far away from home. See Camp Provisions (page 217) for suggested shops.

Bed Role

The sleeping situation is what makes most people shy away from camping, but unless you're going backpacking, you're not limited to a one-pound sleeping pad and bag. Bring whatever fits in your car. (I've been known to pull my down comforter and pillows off my bed, because why not? You can wash the covers!) Futon mattresses can be rolled, sleep like an actual mattress, and don't run the risk of popping in the middle of the night.

Stand and Don't Shiver

Take a cue from early American expeditioners, who traveled long distances with a whole crew. You might not want to haul the 80-pound Civil War–style canvas tents we use, but you can still choose a tent in which you have space to move and stand up.

On a Light Note

Inflatable solar-powered light pods are absolutely amazing. They pack flat, charge in the sun, and give a soft, firefly glow inside the tents. Around the campground, old-school Coleman camping lanterns give off the best light. Battery-powered fairy lights are lovely for draping on the trees.

The Forest Flooring

For a cozy feel, place a big jute rug on the bottom of your tent; it won't stain or hold on to dirt. If you're less ambitious, bring lighter plastic or grass mats that pack down easily.

Swell Decor

It's a major fail if you don't have enough chairs for everyone around the campfire, so start there. Consider a portable awning to provide shade. I love to take furniture camping, as well, whether it's creating a seating area, bringing an ottoman into the tent for discarded clothes, or setting out a small table with removable legs to create a surface for magazines, a glass of wine, or a book.

Fie, Wi-Fi!

Go somewhere that doesn't have Wi-Fi or cell service, so no one is Instagramming, or Facebooking, or e-mailing. It really changes the dynamic.

Dutch Oven Roast Chicken

Comfort food goes over big in the boonies, and the undisputed queen of the genre is the humble roast chicken. Season your bird at home with a simple smoked paprika spice mix, then once on-site, just add a few vegetables and cast-iron alchemy will do the rest. **Serves 4**

One 5-pound chicken, trussed
Kosher salt and freshly ground pepper
1 small lemon, cut into 4 wedges
8 sprigs fresh thyme, plus 1 teaspoon minced fresh thyme leaves
8 sprigs fresh rosemary
2 teaspoons smoked paprika
1½ pounds baby potatoes, halved
8 cipollini onions, halved
2 bunches small rainbow carrots, halved lengthwise
4 tablespoons extra-virgin olive oil
2 tablespoons unsalted butter
6 large garlic cloves, smashed

At Home

1. Pat your bird dry. Salt and pepper the cavity, then stuff with lemon wedges and 4 sprigs each of the thyme and rosemary. In a small bowl, combine 2 tablespoons salt, 1 tablespoon pepper, the smoked paprika, and the minced thyme, then rub it all over the chicken. Wrap the chicken snugly in plastic wrap, place in a resealable plastic bag, and refrigerate for up to 24 hours. Transport in a cooler filled with ice.

At the Campout

2. Prepare a campfire (see page 24).

3. In a mixing bowl, toss the potatoes, cipollini onions, and carrots with 2 tablespoons of the olive oil and a generous sprinkle of salt and pepper.

4. Heat a 12-inch cast-iron Dutch oven over the coals until very hot but not smoking. Add the remaining 2 tablespoons olive oil and the butter, then add the chicken, breast down, and sear until the breast is golden brown, 3 to 4 minutes. Flip the chicken over, put the lid on the Dutch oven, and bake at 450°F (11 coals below the oven, 19 on the lid) for 30 minutes, rotating both the oven and the lid halfway through to avoid hot spots.

5. Carefully remove the oven lid and position the vegetables around the chicken, layering the potatoes first, then the onions, carrots, remaining herbs, and garlic. Replace the lid and cook until the thickest part of the chicken thigh registers 165°F on a meat thermometer,

In the Backpack

- ☐ 12-inch cast-iron Dutch oven
- ☐ Meat thermometer
- ☐ Barbecue tongs
- ☐ Serving platter
- ☐ Foil
- ☐ Carving knife

about 30 minutes more, rotating both the oven and the lid halfway through. Remove the Dutch oven from the coals, transfer the vegetables to a serving platter, and top with the chicken. Tent the chicken with foil, let it rest for 15 minutes, carve, and serve.

tiny tip: If using a smaller Dutch oven, or roasting a bigger chicken, cook the vegetables separately in a foil packet (see page 73).

Four-Cheese, Fennel, and Lamb Bolognese Lasagna

There are certain creature comforts you must do without in the wilderness, like your dishwasher and iPhone-controlled instant pot, but you shall *not* be deprived of lasagna on our watch. This hearty cast-iron cooked version is easy to assemble on-site, using pre-prepped sauce, pre-grated cheese, and the magic of no-boil noodles. **Serves 6**

2 tablespoons extra-virgin olive oil

½ pound ground lamb (see Tiny Tip)

½ pound ground mild Italian sausage

Kosher salt and freshly ground pepper

1 medium onion, diced

4 large garlic cloves, minced

2 teaspoons fennel seeds

Three 14.5-ounce cans puréed tomatoes

¼ cup tomato paste

1 tablespoon chopped fresh oregano

1 teaspoon chopped fresh rosemary

1 teaspoon anchovy paste

½ cup red wine

1 large egg

One 15-ounce container ricotta cheese

One 10-ounce package frozen chopped spinach, thawed, drained, and squeezed dry

4 ounces Pecorino Romano cheese, grated

1 pound whole-milk mozzarella cheese, grated

12 no-boil lasagna noodles, preferably Barilla

2 ounces Parmesan cheese, preferably Parmigiano-Reggiano, grated

At Home

1. Heat the olive oil in a large enameled Dutch oven over medium-high heat until shimmering. Brown the lamb and sausage, and season with a generous pinch each of salt and pepper. Add the onion, garlic, and fennel seeds and cook, stirring, until the onion is soft, about 10 minutes. Mix in the tomato purée, then the tomato paste, oregano, rosemary, 1 teaspoon salt, ¼ teaspoon pepper, the anchovy paste, and the wine. Simmer for 30 minutes, then let cool.

2. Beat the egg in a large bowl, then mix in the ricotta, spinach, 2 ounces of the Pecorino Romano, and a generous pinch each of salt and pepper. In a separate bowl, toss the grated mozzarella with the remaining 2 ounces Pecorino Romano. Transfer the sauce, ricotta mixture, and mixed cheeses to separate resealable containers, and refrigerate.

At the Campout

3. Prepare a campfire (see page 24).

4. Pour one-third of the sauce into the bottom of a 12-inch cast-iron Dutch oven. Break the noodles in half and layer 7 pieces in a circle, overlapping slightly, then place 1 more piece in the center. Spread half the ricotta mixture on top, then one-third of the mixed cheeses. Repeat once more with 8 noodle pieces, then top the mixed cheeses with a third layer of noodles, the remaining sauce, and the remaining mixed cheeses. Sprinkle evenly with the Parmigiano-Reggiano and put on

2 tablespoons finely
chopped fresh
flat-leaf parsley
Cracked pepper

In the Backpack

- ☐ 12-inch cast-iron
  Dutch oven
- ☐ Spatula
- ☐ Serving spoon

the Dutch oven lid. Bake at 375°F (9 coals under the oven, 18 coals on the lid) until hot, bubbling, and easily pierced with a knife, 35 to 45 minutes, rotating both the oven and the lid every 15 minutes or so to avoid hot spots. Let cool slightly, sprinkle with the parsley and cracked pepper, and serve.

tiny tip: If lamb's not your jam, swap in ground beef, turkey, or more sausage.

Be Still, My Stomach: An Ode to Underberg

Sometimes one's stomach goes on strike at the least opportune time, like when one is two Danner boots deep in a remote Glacier National Park meadow, approximately 100 miles and 100 grizzly bears away from the nearest Pepto purveyor. In trying times like these, turn to Underberg, a mysterious bottled German-born blend of herb bitters that comes tightly swaddled in its own miniature brown paper bag. This discreet and diminutive digestif's directions are as straightforward as they are explicit: "Not to be sipped, but taken all at once and quickly because of its aromatic strong taste." So go right ahead and overindulge in *Chorizo Skillet Nachos* (page 98)—just make sure someone's wearing the official Underberg Bitters Belt, which can hold up to twenty bottles at a time.

Middle-of-Nowhere Mac 'n' Beer Cheese

We never feel guilty about eating the decadent beer cheese that hails from our dear friends at the world's finest sausage slingers, Olympia Provisions. It's a melty wonder that takes any classic Americana dish to the next level, whether drizzled on a Frito Pie (see page 109), a hot dog, a pudgie pie (see page 96), or a breakfast burrito (see page 198) or used as a dip for warm, soft, freshly baked pretzels. Bring this beer cheese solo for various camp uses, or bake with elbow noodles for a mac 'n' cheese with an outrageous goo factor. **Makes 3 cups beer cheese; serves 4 for Mac 'n' Beer Cheese**

Beer Cheese
1 cup heavy cream
1 cup whole milk
1 cup beer (preferably Old German)
1 white onion, finely diced
2 tablespoons cornstarch
10 ounces American cheese, cut into pieces
4 ounces white cheddar cheese, grated
Pinch of freshly grated nutmeg
Kosher salt and freshly ground pepper

Mac 'n' Beer Cheese
12 ounces elbow macaroni
2 tablespoons unsalted butter
¾ cup panko bread crumbs
1 cup shredded Monterey Jack

In the Backpack
☐ Cast-iron skillet
☐ 10-inch cast-iron Dutch oven
☐ Serving spoon

At Home

1. To make the beer cheese: Combine the cream, milk, beer, and onion in a large saucepan. Bring to a boil over medium-high heat, then reduce the heat to maintain a simmer and cook for 5 minutes.

2. Using a fork, combine the cornstarch and ¼ cup of the hot cream mixture in a small bowl to make a slurry. Add the slurry to the saucepan and bring back to a boil to thicken. Reduce the heat to maintain a simmer and cook, stirring regularly, for 10 minutes.

3. Stir in the American cheese and white cheddar, ¼ cup at a time, letting each addition melt before adding the next. Add the nutmeg, strain the sauce through a fine-mesh sieve, and season with salt and pepper. (If using as a dip, stop here. Pack the beer cheese in a resealable container and reheat on low heat before serving.)

4. To make the Mac 'n' Beer Cheese: Cook the macaroni 2 minutes shy of the package instructions. (Otherwise, it will turn to mush when you bake it.) Drain and combine with the beer cheese. Pack in a resealable gallon-size bag or container and pack the butter, panko, and Monterey Jack in separate small containers. Transport in a cooler filled with ice.

At the Campout

5. Prepare a campfire (see page 24). Melt the butter in a cast-iron skillet over low heat. Stir in the panko to coat and set aside. Plop the noodles and beer cheese in a 10-inch cast-iron Dutch oven and smooth the top with a spoon, top evenly with layers of buttery panko and the shredded cheese, and cover with the lid. Bake at 350°F (7 coals below the oven, 14 on the lid) until the top is golden, about 20 minutes. Serve while hot and gooey.

tiny tip: For a sweet side dish, make mini mac 'n' cheese mugs. Divide the cheesy noodles among six enamel mugs and bake in the Dutch oven.

One-Pouch Saltwater Wonders

Fancy and foil need not be mutually exclusive—this trio of sea-inspired, coal-fired packets is just as sapid as froufrou fish house fare, albeit with more aluminum and fewer white tablecloths. Seafood is particularly well suited to steam cooking and takes less time than poultry or red meat—just layer ingredients in the packets in the order listed, season with salt and pepper to taste, bake in the embers for 10 to 15 minutes, then serve with a green salad, a loaf of fresh sourdough, and crisp Sancerre (or a bucket of iced Corona). If you forgot the foil but are carting cast iron, or would rather simmer a *fresh*water swimmer, paddle along to the next recipe, Skillet-Fried Rainbow Trout with Lemon and Fresh Dill (page 124). **Serves 1**

Tinfoil Shrimp Boil

3 small red potatoes, quartered
⅛ onion, diced
½ ear of corn, kernels removed
½ ear of corn, cut into
   three rounds
5 raw unpeeled extra-jumbo
   shrimp
Eight ½-inch rounds kielbasa,
   cut diagonally
¼ cup lager-style beer
1 tablespoon unsalted butter
2 teaspoons Old Bay seasoning
1 tablespoon snipped
   fresh chives

Mountaineers' Meunière

1 cup spinach
¼ leek, thinly sliced
1 sole fillet
4 paper-thin lemon slices
6 asparagus spears
1 sprig fresh dill
1 tablespoon olive oil
1 tablespoon white wine

Spindrift Scallops

1 baby bok choy, halved
2 ounces shiitake or enoki
   mushrooms
6 large scallops
1 teaspoon grated fresh ginger
2 teaspoons toasted
   sesame oil
1 teaspoon soy sauce
1 teaspoon fresh lime juice
3 fresh cilantro sprigs

The Littlest Campers

If you happen to find yourself in a life stage when your primary responsibilities go to bed as the sun goes down and yet you cannot leave them, you might find yourself wondering where to go on vacation. Might we suggest a campout? Everyone has a blast when the entertainment is provided, the shelter quite affordable, and the menu attuned to every party's particularities. After turndown, kids and adults can have their own fun, whether in the tent or at the campfire just outside it. Take to heart the following advice from experienced parents and clear a trail to family-camping success.

- There's clean, and then there's campout clean. Leave germophobia at home, and embrace the boost your collective immune system will receive from life with little soap.

- Ease transitions by using packing cubes to organize everyone's clothing and gear by activity— group swim gear, hiking outfits, and pajamas—rather than by person.

- Keep 'em entertained with dominoes, cards, and board games that can spare missing pieces. Cornhole and ladderball even the playing field for all ages. And for larger gatherings, you can't beat the enthusiasm for capture the flag or kickball.

- As in day-to-day parenting, snacks are the key to happiness. Try this Toddler Trex Mix: Throw together equal parts sliced almonds, peanut butter puffs, teddy bear–shaped graham crackers, dehydrated blueberries, and apple rings.

- Bring extras of everything, particularly diapers, wipes/Wet-Naps, swimsuits (so there's always a dry one available), and socks.

- Stick to your bedtime routine as much as possible to discourage overly early risers. In the case of crib sleepers, set up a travel crib inside the tent.

- If you see a flashlight flicker under a sleeping bag, turn a blind eye. That's childhood-memory gold.

- If there's great interest in staying up overly late, set all clocks, watches, and phones ahead and feign exhaustion at "midnight."

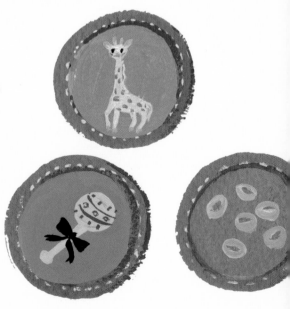

Skillet-Fried Rainbow Trout with Lemon and Fresh Dill

If fishing's on your itinerary, this will be a true stream-to-skillet meal; otherwise, pick up trout at your neighborhood fishmonger. Before you buy, check for signs that your swimmers are spanking fresh—clear, slightly bulging eyes; firm and shiny flesh; dark red gills; and the absence of eau de fish. **Serves 4**

4 whole trout, gutted
Kosher salt and freshly
    ground pepper
2 lemons, thinly sliced
1 bunch fresh dill
2 tablespoons unsalted
    butter
2 tablespoons extra-virgin
    olive oil
Fresh herbs, for garnish

In the Backpack

☐ Two 12-inch cast-iron
    skillets
☐ Kitchen twine
☐ Barbecue tongs
☐ Serving platter

1. Prepare a campfire (see page 24) and fit it with a grill grate, or set up the camp stove. Heat two 12-inch cast-iron skillets on the campfire grill grate or on the camp stove over medium-high heat until hot but not smoking, about 10 minutes.

2. Liberally sprinkle the inside of each trout with salt and pepper. Line the cavity with lemon slices (about 3 slices per fish), then stuff with a handful of fresh dill sprigs. Gently tie each fish shut with 8-inch lengths of kitchen twine (also about 3 per fish).

3. Put the butter and olive oil in the hot skillet and gently swirl to mix. Add 2 fish to each skillet and cook, undisturbed, for about 3 minutes per side, until the skin is crisp and the flesh is soft and flaky. Transfer the fish to a platter and garnish with whole fresh herbs and the remaining lemon slices.

How to Clean a Fish

For the freshest fish-fry possible, clean your trout as soon as you conclude your riverbank victory dance.

1. Lay the fish on its side and use the tip of a very sharp paring knife to cut through the skin along the belly, from the anus to just below the fish's jaws.

2. Gently pull out the fish's gills and entrails, then scrape off the blood vein that runs along the spine.

3. Rinse the trout several times in cold water, then cook immediately, or wrap in plastic wrap and store directly on ice.

Bone-In Pork Chops with Fresh Sage, Onions, and Apples

After a long day on the lake, few things are as satisfying as a thick, juicy pork chop, especially one smothered in roasted apples and sage. During peak stone-fruit season, switch out the apples and onions for ripe peach halves, searing them with the sage until tender and beginning to caramelize. **Makes 4**

Sage-Coffee Rub
2 tablespoons kosher salt
1 tablespoon freshly ground
    pepper
1 teaspoon finely ground
    coffee beans
1 teaspoon garlic powder
1 teaspoon paprika
1 teaspoon dried rubbed
    sage

Pork Chops
4 bone-in rib chops
    (1½ inches thick)
3 tablespoons unsalted
    butter
2 tablespoons canola oil
1 small yellow onion,
    thinly sliced
3 medium Honeycrisp,
    Fuji, or Gala apples,
    cut into 16 pieces each
10 fresh sage leaves

At Home
1. To make the rub: Combine the salt, pepper, coffee, garlic powder, paprika, and sage in a 4-ounce Mason jar and shake to mix.

At the Campout
2. To make the pork chops: Pat the pork chops dry and sprinkle the rub evenly over both sides, pressing gently to adhere. Let the chops sit at room temperature for 30 to 45 minutes.

3. Prepare a campfire (see page 24) and fit it with a grill grate, or set up the camp stove. Heat two 12-inch cast-iron skillets on the campfire grill grate or on the camp stove over medium-high heat until very hot but not smoking, about 10 minutes.

4. Put 1 tablespoon of the butter and 1 tablespoon of the canola oil in each skillet, swirling to mix, then add 2 chops to each skillet and cook until medium-rare, about 10 minutes per side. Check the internal temperature with a meat thermometer; the chops are done when they reach 145°F.

In the Backpack

- Two 12-inch cast-iron skillets
- Meat thermometer
- Barbecue tongs
- Foil
- Steak knives

5. When the chops are cooked through, transfer them to a plate and tent with foil. While they rest, combine the remaining 1 tablespoon butter, the onion, apples, and fresh sage in one of the hot skillets. Cook, stirring occasionally, until the onion is soft and the apples are slightly caramelized, about 10 minutes. Plate the pork chops, pouring any juices from the plate over the top. Divide the apple-onion-sage mixture evenly among the plates and serve.

Bootstrap Bibimbap

One of our favorite grillables, *galbi* ribs, is also one of the most portable—just slip the meaty bones in a bag with an Asian pear and soy–infused marinade, and tote them with you to the timberline. Make them the main course, or make them the main act in this supremely satisfying bibimbap bowl, which rounds out the meal with pickles, sweet potato glass noodles, rice, spinach, kimchi, and an egg. **Serves 4**

Gochujang Sauce
¼ cup gochujang
    (Korean chile paste)
2 tablespoons soy sauce
1 tablespoon sugar
1 tablespoon rice vinegar
1 tablespoon toasted
    sesame oil
3 large garlic cloves, minced
2 teaspoons sesame seeds

Pickles
3 Persian cucumbers, sliced
    paper thin
½ teaspoon kosher salt
¼ cup soy sauce
2 teaspoons toasted
    sesame oil
1 teaspoon minced fresh
    ginger

Noodles
8 ounces dried sweet
    potato glass noodles
    (often sold as Korean
    vermicelli)

Short Ribs
Galbi Marinade (see page 61)
2 pounds short ribs, or
    3 per person (cut flanken-
    style, in ½-inch-thick
    slices across the bones)

1½ cups sushi rice
2 tablespoons canola oil
2 garlic cloves, minced
Two 5-ounce bags raw
    baby spinach
¼ cup sesame seeds
4 large eggs

At Home
1. To make the gochujang sauce: Whisk together all the sauce ingredients with ¼ cup water in a medium bowl, transfer to an 8-ounce Mason jar, and refrigerate.

2. To make the pickles: Toss the cucumbers with the salt in a large bowl, let sit for 20 minutes, then drain. Mix the soy sauce, sesame oil, and ginger in a small jar and add 1 tablespoon of the mixture to the sliced cucumbers, reserving the rest. Transfer the cucumbers to a resealable container and refrigerate.

3. To make the noodles: In a medium saucepan, cook the sweet potato noodles according to the directions on the package, then drain and rinse with cold water. Toss the noodles with the soy-sesame-ginger mixture reserved in step 2 and transfer to a resealable container and refrigerate.

4. To make the short ribs: Prepare the Galbi Marinade, pour it into a gallon-size resealable bag, add the ribs, and seal. Shake, rattle, and roll until the ribs are completely covered. Marinate in the refrigerator for at least 4 hours, but preferably overnight.

At the Campout
5. Prepare a campfire (see page 24) and fit it with a grill grate. Set up the camp stove.

6. In a medium saucepan, cook the rice on the camp stove according to the directions on the package (or skip this step and pack in take-out rice).

1 large carrot, coarsely
   shredded
2 cups bean sprouts
One 14-ounce jar kimchi

In the Backpack

- ☐ Medium saucepan
- ☐ 12-inch cast-iron skillet
- ☐ Mixing bowl
- ☐ Barbecue tongs
- ☐ Platter
- ☐ Four large serving bowls

7. Heat 1 tablespoon of the canola oil in a 12-inch cast-iron skillet over medium-high heat on the camp stove, then add garlic and cook for 30 seconds. Add the spinach in batches and cook, stirring, until wilted, 2 to 3 minutes. Sprinkle with half the sesame seeds, transfer to a bowl, and set aside.

8. Cook the short ribs over medium-high heat on the campfire grill grate, about 3 minutes per side. Transfer to a platter and sprinkle with the remaining sesame seeds. Meanwhile, return the skillet to the camp stove, add the remaining 1 tablespoon canola oil, and fry the eggs. While they're frying, divide the rice and sweet potato noodles among four large bowls and top with the spinach, carrots, bean sprouts, cucumbers, and kimchi. Divide the galbi ribs evenly among the bowls. Top each bowl with a fried egg and serve with the gochujang sauce and extra kimchi. Set out an extra bowl for the discarded bones.

Compound Butters: The Incomparable Camp Cooking Companion

Prep these sweet and savory infused butters at home in mere minutes, then use them to flavor everything from ember-baked potatoes (see page 74) and corn on the cob (see page 70) to grilled rib-eye steaks (see page 132). Or, particularly in the case of the Cinnamon–Brown Sugar Butter, just eat it straight from the jar with a spork; the squirrels won't tell.

Cinnamon–Brown Sugar

2 teaspoons ground cinnamon
¼ cup packed dark brown sugar
¼ teaspoon pure vanilla extract
⅛ teaspoon kosher salt

Spicy Roasted Garlic

1 head garlic, roasted (see Tiny Tip), cloves peeled
1 tablespoon minced fresh flat-leaf parsley
½ teaspoon red pepper flakes
½ teaspoon kosher salt

Gremolata

2 teaspoons lemon zest
1 tablespoon finely chopped fresh flat-leaf parsley
1 large garlic clove, minced
½ teaspoon kosher salt

Shallot-Herb

¼ cup minced shallots
2 tablespoons minced fresh flat-leaf parsley
2 tablespoons minced fresh thyme
2 tablespoons minced fresh tarragon
½ teaspoon kosher salt

Chili-Lime

1 teaspoon chili powder
2 teaspoons grated lime zest
½ teaspoon kosher salt

Smoked Paprika–Garlic

1 teaspoon smoked paprika
1 tablespoon minced garlic
½ teaspoon kosher salt

Smoosh Like So
Start with 8 tablespoons (1 stick) softened unsalted butter, and mix in the seasonings with a fork or in a food processor. Transfer the compound butter to a widemouthed 8-ounce Mason jar and refrigerate until there's a reason for the season. Butters will keep for about 2 weeks in the refrigerator and up to 3 months in the freezer.

---

tiny tip: To roast a head of garlic, trim ¼ inch off the top, drizzle with 1 teaspoon olive oil, wrap in foil, and bake in a 400°F oven for 40 minutes until soft.

Camp Cookery Kit

Stock a tackle box with the following foodstuffs, and you'll be ready to flee civilization at a moment's notice, without sacrificing the essentials (i.e., coffee cake and bourbon).

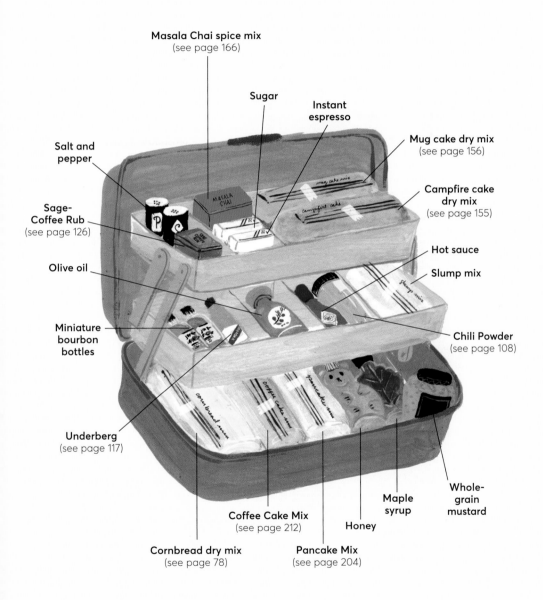

Masala Chai spice mix
(see page 166)

Sugar

Instant espresso

Mug cake dry mix
(see page 156)

Salt and pepper

Campfire cake dry mix
(see page 155)

Sage-Coffee Rub
(see page 126)

Hot sauce

Olive oil

Slump mix

Miniature bourbon bottles

Chili Powder
(see page 108)

Underberg
(see page 117)

Whole-grain mustard

Maple syrup

Coffee Cake Mix
(see page 212)

Honey

Cornbread dry mix
(see page 78)

Pancake Mix
(see page 204)

Big Sky Rib-Eye with Shallot-Herb Butter

Nothing fortifies a famished camper quite like a huge hunk of seared red meat, especially when it's topped with a rich shallot-and-herb-infused butter. If you can't bear to toss the bones after dinner, save them for making bone broth or stock, and if for some reason you have leftover meat, plan on steak 'n' eggs or steak hash for breakfast. **Serves 4**

Shallot-Herb Butter
    (page 130)
Four 1½-inch-thick bone-in
    rib-eye steaks
Kosher salt and freshly
    ground pepper

In the Backpack

☐ 12-inch cast-iron skillet
☐ Barbecue tongs
☐ Meat thermometer
☐ Steak knives

At Home

1. Prepare the Shallot-Herb Butter and refrigerate.

At the Campout

2. Remove the steaks from the cooler, pat dry, and season liberally with salt and pepper (about 1 teaspoon salt per steak and pepper to taste). Let the steaks rest until they come to room temperature, about 45 minutes, and pat dry again.

3. Prepare a campfire (see page 24) and fit it with a grill grate, or set up the camp stove.

4. Heat a 12-inch cast-iron skillet on the campfire grill grate or on the camp stove over medium-high heat until hot but not smoking, about 10 minutes. Add the rib-eyes (1 or 2 at a time, depending on size—don't crowd the pan). For medium-rare, sear for about 5 minutes per side, or until the internal temperature reaches 130° to 135°F.

5. Plate the steaks and top each with a generous dollop of Shallot-Herb Butter. Let rest for 10 minutes to allow the juices to settle, then serve.

In a Clinch: A Love Story

Sometimes dropping your steak in the coals is for the best—when you're clinching, that is. Also known as "dirty grilling," clinching is the practice of cooking a fat, juicy, majestically marbled steak directly on hot coals, and it has long been popular with cowboys, ranchers, and pro grillers. In fact, even the inimitable Julia Child was known to clinch every now and then—her hunk of choice was a rib-eye roast.

The premise behind clinching is simple: Build a fire with high-quality lump charcoal (made with hot-burning hardwood), season your steak as desired, firmly tamp down a suitably sized bed of campfire coals with a skillet or Dutch oven, use your dog-eared copy of *Wild* to fan any ashes off the coals until they glow white hot (just the coals, not the book), then take a deep breath and let go of your rib-eye, because if you love something clinched, you have to set it free. (If you're particularly anxious, you can always lay a cross-wire cooling rack over the coals and grill on that.)

Much like when two people are highly attracted to each other, the meat and heat instantaneously enter into a wildly passionate clinch, completely excluding any flames from their little tête-à-tête. When the two are finally parted (after 2 to 4 minutes per side for a medium-rare affair), dust off any residual ash, slice, and serve, perhaps with Sautéed Chanterelle Mushrooms (page 69) or Garlicky Grilled Artichokes (page 68). Talk about a storybook ending!

Road-tripping to all fifty-nine national parks in person is a lifelong endeavor, but experiencing them in hot dog form can be done in the span of a single campout. Here's a sampling of twelve regionally influenced, thematically topped wieners that will whet both your wanderlust *and* your appetite.

1. Yellowstone: All-beef (or anything but bison, really) dog, yellow mustard, geysers of ketchup, supervolcanically spicy relish, potato bun

2. Acadia: Red snapper hot dog, lobster salad, chopped chives, crumbled Humpty Dumpty potato chips, New England–style hot dog roll

3. Carlsbad Caverns: Spicy chorizo dog, chipotle mayonnaise, roasted Hatch green chiles, calabacitas, red *and* green chile sauce, crumbled chicharrones, sopaipilla bun

4. Saguaro (aka the "Sonoran" Dog): Bacon-wrapped frank, grilled and raw onions, pinto beans, pico de gallo, mayonnaise, yellow mustard, jalapeño sauce, split-top bolillo roll

5. Hawaii Volcanoes: Wild boar hot dog, teriyaki mayonnaise, grilled pineapple, spicy mango relish, King's Hawaiian hot dog bun

Hot Dog Homage: Our National Parks in 12 Tantalizing Toppers

6. Crater Lake: Bratwurst, beer mustard, beer cheese, warm chanterelles, pork belly cracklings, chopped hazelnuts, brioche bun

7. Denali: Reindeer sausage, Moosetard, giant cabbage slaw, wild smoked salmon candy bits, sourdough bun

8. Olympic: Wild venison sausage, smoked oyster cream cheese, apple slaw, grilled Walla Walla onions, steelhead roe, classic bun

9. Cuyahoga Valley: Polish dog, French fries, sweet barbecue sauce, coleslaw, classic bun

10. Great Smoky Mountains: Red Hot dog, ground beef chili, coleslaw, chopped raw onions, yellow mustard, steamed bun

11. Isle Royale: Vienna sausage, beef heart chili, diced raw onions, yellow mustard, classic bun

12. Joshua Tree: Hot dog on a stick, squiggle of yellow mustard

Chapter 5

S'mores and More

Sitting round the fire after a particularly scrumptious camp supper, it's hard to imagine taking even one more bite . . . until the s'mores fixings come out. While we humbly acknowledge that marvelous, time-tested mash-up of graham crackers, marshmallows, and melted chocolate as the reigning camp dessert queen, here are plenty of other sweets fit for firelight, from slabs of crisp, crunchy Salted Honey-Maple Peanut Brittle to Coal-Baked Apples with Cinnamon-Cider Sauce and a drizzle of cream. And since you'll be dreaming of Brown Butter Toffee Blondies and Banana Boats long into the night, you won't even hear the coyotes howling.

S'mores Galores

Mix, match, and melt with this sky's-the-limit s'moregasbord, which pairs the requisite marshmallow with fun store-bought (and often chocolate-laden) substitutions for ordinary grahams. (For extraordinary *homemade* grahams, see page 142.) Distinguish yourself as a professional roaster by pre-melting your chocolate atop the cracker on a toasty nearby log or on the grill grate while you roast your marshmallow. By the time you smoosh everything together, the melt factor will be off the charts.

S'miscuits
Chocolate digestive biscuits + crumbled Salted Honey-Maple Peanut Brittle (page 149) + raw honey

S'moreos
Oreo Thins + hot fudge sauce + sprinkles

S'moolboys
Le Petit Écolier (70% Cocoa) "Schoolboy" cookies + Dark Rum Caramel (page 144) + crushed pretzels

S'mobnobs
Hobnobs + Nutella + sliced strawberries

S'mortbreads
Shortbread rounds + lemon curd + raspberries

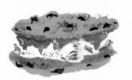

S'mocolates
Tate's chocolate chip cookies +
cherry jam + crushed smoked almonds

S'mackers
Cinnamon graham crackers +
peanut butter cup + banana slices

S'mamoas
Samoas + Dark Rum Caramel (page 144) +
crushed macadamia nuts

S'mafers
Chocolate wafers + marmalade +
crushed pistachios

S'maps
Gingersnaps + passion fruit curd +
toasted coconut flakes

S'milanos
Milanos + Andes Mints +
chocolate sprinkles

S'moopwafels
Stroopwafels + blackberry jam +
smoked honey

Vanilla Bean Dream Marshmallows & Co.

If you've never made a marshmallow, brace for magic. This uncomplicated confection comes together with very little effort—just make sure you've got a candy thermometer, and a dance routine to keep yourself alert during the inactive bits. These marvelous marshmallows are pillowy enough to enjoy straight from the pan and strong enough to stay on your stick; we recommend you make a few flavors at home, freeze them, then ferry them to the campfire in your cooler to avoid untimely melting on hot summer days. **Makes 36**

Nonstick cooking spray
Three ¼-ounce packets unflavored powdered gelatin
1 vanilla bean, split lengthwise and seeds scraped out, or 1 teaspoon vanilla bean paste
2 teaspoons pure vanilla extract
1½ cups granulated sugar
1 cup light corn syrup
¼ teaspoon kosher salt
¼ cup cornstarch
¼ cup confectioners' sugar

In the Backpack

☐ Roasting sticks

1. Line a 9-by-9-inch metal cake pan with parchment paper, leaving an overhang on two opposite sides of the pan, and generously spray with nonstick cooking spray.

2. In the bowl of a stand mixer fitted with the whisk attachment, mix the gelatin and ½ cup water on low speed until blended together, about 15 seconds. In a small bowl, mix the vanilla seeds into the vanilla extract and set aside.

3. In a 2-quart saucepan, stir together ½ cup water, the granulated sugar, corn syrup, and salt over medium heat. Bring to a boil and cook, without stirring, until a candy thermometer reads 240°F, 15 to 20 minutes. Remove the pan from the heat and, with the mixer on low speed, slowly pour the syrup into the gelatin mixture. Increase the speed to high and continue mixing until the marshmallow is fluffy and glossy and holds a soft peak, about 15 minutes. Add the vanilla mixture and mix for 1 minute more. Pour the mixture into the prepared pan and smooth the surface using wet fingers or a rubber spatula dipped in water. Let set at room temperature for at least 8 hours, but preferably overnight.

4. In a large bowl, sift together the cornstarch and confectioners' sugar. Remove the marshmallows from the baking dish using the overhanging parchment paper as handles. Sprinkle the marshmallows liberally with the cornstarch mixture, then dip a sharp knife in the cornstarch mixture and cut the marshmallows into 1½-inch squares. Toss them in the cornstarch mixture (this prevents stickiness) and transfer to an airtight container, placing parchment paper between layers. Roast immediately, or store at room temperature for up to 2 weeks or in the freezer for up to 3 months.

Marshmallow Variations

Strawberry: Grind 1 ounce freeze-dried strawberries into powder in a food processor and add in place of the vanilla extract and seeds or paste.

Chocolate: Add ¼ cup sifted unsweetened cocoa powder in place of the vanilla extract and seeds or paste, and replace 2 tablespoons of the confectioners' sugar with unsweetened cocoa powder.

Neapolitan: Layer half a batch each of chocolate, vanilla, and strawberry mixture in a 9-by-13-inch metal cake pan, letting the preceding batch set as you make the next.

Coconut: Add 1 teaspoon coconut extract in lieu of the vanilla extract and seeds or paste, and roll the marshmallows in 2 cups toasted unsweetened shredded coconut instead of cornstarch.

Passion Fruit: Replace the ½ cup water in step 2 with strained passion fruit purée, and add 2 tablespoons strained purée in place of the vanilla extract and seeds or paste.

Mango: Replace the ½ cup water in step 2 with strained mango purée, and add 2 tablespoons strained mango purée in place of the vanilla extract and seeds or paste.

Matcha: Add 1 tablespoon matcha powder in place of the vanilla extract and seeds or paste.

Raspberry Rose Water: Replace the ½ cup water in step 2 with raspberry purée, and add ½ teaspoon rose water in place of the vanilla extract and seeds or paste.

Bourbon Vanilla: Add 1 tablespoon bourbon when you add the vanilla.

Peppermint: Add 1 teaspoon pure peppermint extract in place of the vanilla extract and seeds or paste, and after smoothing the mixture in the pan, add 12 drops of natural red food dye and use a chopstick to quickly marble.

Champagne: Replace the water in steps 2 and 3 with chilled champagne (or rosé), omit the vanilla extract and seeds or paste, and for extra bling, dust the finished marshmallows with gold sprinkles.

Golden Graham Crackers

These crispy cousins of the store-bought graham crackers we idolized as kids are a snap to make *and* eat. While their ultimate destiny is to bookend slabs of melted chocolate and homemade marshmallows as part of the perfect s'more, they're also delectable dipped in nut butters, chocolate hazelnut spread, and Peanut Butter Hot Chocolate (page 168). **Makes about 30**

1½ cups whole wheat pastry flour
½ cup all-purpose flour, plus more for dusting
⅓ cup packed dark brown sugar
½ teaspoon baking powder
½ teaspoon baking soda
½ teaspoon kosher salt
1 teaspoon ground cinnamon
6 tablespoons (¾ stick) chilled unsalted butter, cut into cubes
3 tablespoons whole milk
1 teaspoon pure vanilla extract
3 tablespoons honey
1 tablespoon molasses

tiny tip: If for some strange reason you have leftovers, freeze them to use for future graham cracker crusts.

1. Preheat the oven to 325°F. Line two rimmed baking sheets with parchment paper.

2. In a food processor, pulse together the whole wheat flour, all-purpose flour, brown sugar, baking powder, baking soda, salt, and cinnamon. Add the butter and pulse until the mixture resembles coarse meal. Whisk together the milk, vanilla, honey, and molasses in a medium bowl until smooth. Pour over the dry ingredients in the food processor and pulse just until the dough comes together. Transfer the dough to a floured surface, knead to bring it together, then shape into a square. Wrap in plastic wrap and refrigerate for 30 minutes.

3. Remove the dough from the refrigerator and split it in half. On a lightly floured surface, roll each half into a ⅛-inch-thick rectangle (the thinner you can get the dough, the crispier the crackers will be). Using a pastry wheel and a ruler, cut the dough into 2½-inch squares (or 2½-by-5-inch rectangles, to mimic the store-bought version) and set them on the prepared baking sheets. Gather the scraps, chill them, and reroll. Prick the crackers with a fork or skewer and chill in the refrigerator for 15 minutes. Bake until crisp and golden, 15 to 18 minutes. Cool completely, then store the crackers in an airtight container for up to 1 week, or freeze for up to 3 months.

MENU

Big Night, by Starlight

Gather round the fire, break out the Camp-ari, and make a big night of it.

Garlicky Grilled Artichokes 68

Summer Squash, Snap Pea, and Asparagus Salad 90

Ember-Baked Cipollini Onions 74

Roasted Garlic Parmesan Monkey Bread 77

**Four-Cheese, Fennel, and
Lamb Bolognese Lasagna** 116

**Chocolate Raspberry Caramel
Fire Ban S'mores** 145

Badlands Boulevardier 161

Camp-ari Cup Jelly Shot 177

Dark Rum Caramel

Destined to be drizzled over grilled freestone peaches and juicy just-picked berries, this boozy caramel can also be put to good use as a sundae topping, s'more stuffer, or camp coffee sweetener. Once the sugar turns amber, things get hot and heavy, so have all tools and ingredients at hand and ready to rum-ble. **Makes 1 cup**

⅓ cup heavy cream
3 tablespoons unsalted butter
1 vanilla bean, split and seeds scraped
1 teaspoon pure vanilla extract
¼ teaspoon kosher salt
¾ cup sugar
2 tablespoons dark rum, such as Cruzan

1. Warm the cream, butter, vanilla bean seeds, vanilla extract, and salt in a small saucepan over low heat until the butter is melted, then remove from the heat.

2. In a 2-quart saucepan, mix together the sugar and 3 tablespoons water, then simmer over medium-high heat, without stirring, until the sugar turns amber, 8 to 10 minutes. Turn off the heat, add the cream mixture, and whisk until smooth (the caramel will froth and foam wildly). Whisk in the rum. Let the caramel cool, transfer to an 8-ounce Mason jar, and refrigerate for up to 2 weeks. Rewarm in a saucepan of simmering water before serving.

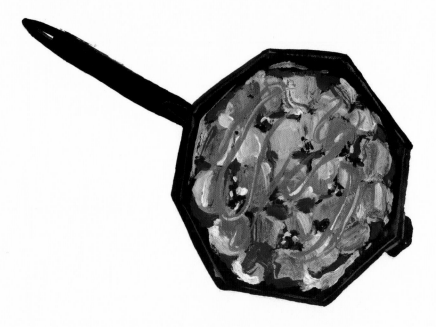

Chocolate Raspberry Caramel Fire Ban S'mores

Also known as S'mores Nachos, these are an exceptional backup plan should a fire ban or severe stick shortage foil your campfire fun. To achieve the toasty marshmallow tops afforded by a home oven, pack the kitchen torch, or pick up an inexpensive torch attachment for your propane tank. **Serves 4**

Golden Graham Crackers (page 142), baked in 1¼-by-2½-inch batons
Chocolate Marshmallows (page 141)
Dark Rum Caramel (page 144)
10 ounces dark or bittersweet chocolate, chopped into ¼-inch pieces
½ cup chopped toasted pecans
1 pint fresh raspberries
2 tablespoons sugar

In the Backpack

☐ Pot
☐ 10-inch cast-iron skillet
☐ Propane torch

At Home

1. Prepare the Golden Graham Crackers, Chocolate Marshmallows, and Dark Rum Caramel and store separately in airtight containers. Combine the chopped chocolate and pecans in a 1-quart Mason jar and gently shake to mix. In a medium bowl, toss the raspberries with the sugar, gently smash with a slotted spoon or spatula until smooth, then transfer to a 1-pint Mason jar and refrigerate.

At the Campout

2. Prepare a campfire (see page 24) and fit it with a grill grate, or set up the camp stove.

3. Remove the raspberry mash from the cooler and let it come to room temperature. Warm the jar of caramel in a saucepan of simmering water until easily pourable. Reserve ½ cup of the chocolate-pecan mixture and pour the rest over the bottom of a 10-inch cast-iron skillet. Layer the raspberry mash evenly over the top, then pour on half the caramel. Add a snug layer of marshmallows, pressing them down gently. Cook on the campfire grill grate or over medium-low heat on the camp stove until warm and melty, about 10 minutes, then use a propane torch to toast the marshmallow tops until golden brown. Sprinkle with the remaining chocolate-pecan mixture, drizzle with the remaining caramel, and serve with the graham cracker batons for dipping.

The Sticking Point:
5 Singular Skewerings

No pan, no problem! All you really need to cook in the woods is a common stick, of which there are nearly as many as there are insects and arachnids hiding under them, so collect with caution. Here's a helpful guide to matching your flame-broiled epicurean endeavor with its stick soul mate.

1. **Curved: Bacon**
   Some people like their bacon burnt and crispy. Others, less so. A gently arching stick allows you to position the bacon at different heights from the fire, so you can sauté and flambé simultaneously.

2. **Forked: Damper**
   Not just the state of your tent on a particularly dewy morning, damper is a traditional Australian traveler's bread made with flour, water, and baking soda. If for some reason this combination doesn't appeal, make our Perfect Pizza Dough (page 101) instead, wind strips of dough around a stout forked stick, and hold it over the coals until the dough is cooked through. When the stick is removed, some people might want to fill the resulting holes with jam, chocolate, or Nutella, and those people are brilliant.

3. Green: Egg

If camping with a real know-it-all, ask if they've ever cooked an egg on a stick. If so, go back to suffering in silence. If not, seize this one-upping opportunity by sharpening a thin green stick, ever so carefully poking a hole in either end of a raw egg, running the stick through the egg, and air-boiling it over the fire. You win.

4. Multibranched: Cherry Tomatoes

The multibranched stick is a particular kind of challenge, but cherry tomatoes rise to the occasion. Thread a few tomatoes on each branch, hold it horizontally over the fire, and wait for the soft pops to start.

5. Straight and Narrow: Grilled Cheese Sandwich

All your life, you've believed that chunks of meat and vegetables belong on a skewer, and grilled cheese sandwiches belong in a skillet. But grilled cheese sandwiches are more versatile than that, and when quartered, threaded vertically on a strong, straight stick, then carefully coal toasted, they'll elicit far more excitement than a prosaic steak, onion, and bell pepper skewer, guaranteed.

Chocolate Popcorn

It would be impossible to improve upon the platonic ideal of kitschy campfire snacks, Jiffy Pop—the popcorn that packs its own theater and provides its own show. If we had our way, we'd issue every camper that portable popcorn roaster on her or his way into the woods. But variety is the spice of camp life, and that's where chocolate popcorn comes in. Make a batch at home on the morning of your departure and mix it 50/50 with your fireside-popped popcorn, or pass it around the car as a pre-campout pump-up. **Makes 3 cups**

1 tablespoon coconut oil
¼ cup mushroom popcorn
  kernels (see Tiny Tips)
¾ cup sugar
½ teaspoon kosher salt
¼ cup unsweetened Dutch-
  processed cocoa powder
  (see Tiny Tips)

tiny tips:
Plump, spherical mushroom popcorn, reminiscent of kettle corn at the state fair, is widely available online.

Dutch-processed cocoa powder is labeled several different ways; to be sure you're getting the right thing, look for this phrase in the ingredients list: "cocoa processed with alkali."

1. Line a baking sheet with parchment paper.

2. Heat the coconut oil and popcorn kernels in a large pot, covered, over medium-high heat. When the first kernel pops, remove from the heat, shake the pot, and return to the heat. Continue shaking every 10 seconds or so until the popping slows, then remove from the heat for good. Shake the popcorn so the unpopped kernels fall out of harm's way, and scoop the popcorn into a large bowl.

3. Combine ¾ cup water, the sugar, and the salt in a medium saucepan and bring to a boil. Cook until a candy thermometer reads 220°F. Stir in the cocoa powder. Cook until the syrup reaches 240°F. Working quickly, pour the syrup over the popcorn and stir to fully incorporate. Spread the popcorn on the prepared baking sheet and break it up as much as possible. Let cool and pack in a gallon-size resealable bag. The popcorn is best eaten within 2 days.

Salted Honey-Maple Peanut Brittle

Much like a whitewater-rafting trip, this recipe starts out quite placidly, then escalates into a thrilling/panicked rush of foam and froth when the baking soda's added. Just keep calm and whisk on—the payoff is an ethereally airy, crunchy brittle that won't last long, because you'll likely eat the entire batch yourself. A word of warning: If you don't have a candy thermometer, go buy one; you're really going to need it.

Makes about fifty 2-by-2-inch pieces

2 cups dry-roasted peanuts (about 10 ounces; see Tiny Tip)
1½ cups sugar
¼ cup honey
¼ cup dark maple syrup
1 tablespoon unsalted butter, melted
1 tablespoon baking soda, sifted
1 teaspoon flaky salt

tiny tip: If you aren't crazy about peanuts, substitute a different nut, or mix and match.

1. Preheat the oven to 200°F. Line a 12-by-18-inch rimmed baking sheet with parchment paper.

2. Spread 1½ cups of the peanuts on the prepared baking sheet, place it in the oven, and turn the oven off. Let warm for 10 minutes. Meanwhile, chop the remaining ½ cup peanuts and set aside. Remove the baking sheet from the oven and transfer the warmed peanuts to a small bowl; set the baking sheet aside.

3. Combine ¼ cup water, the sugar, honey, and maple syrup in a 3-quart saucepan and bring to a boil over medium-high heat. Cook until the caramel registers 275°F on a candy thermometer, then stir in the butter and warmed peanuts. Cook, watching carefully, until the mixture hits 300°F. Turn off the heat, add the baking soda, and stir madly with a spatula for 3 to 5 seconds. Immediately pour the foamy, lumpy mixture down the center of the baking sheet, scraping from the bottom of the saucepan with the spatula as you go, to distribute the peanuts evenly. The mixture should settle down and spread out—resist smoothing it, or it will deflate.

4. Immediately sprinkle the chopped peanuts and flaky salt evenly over the surface and let the brittle sit until fully hardened, at least 1 hour. Break into pieces and store in an airtight container for up to 2 weeks.

Brown Butter Toffee Blondies

The only trick to acing toffee is pulling it off the heat at the right moment. Enlist a candy thermometer, and the Wonka badge will be yours in no time. **Makes 24**

Toffee
¾ cup granulated sugar
¾ cup (1½ sticks) unsalted butter
⅛ teaspoon kosher salt
½ cup semisweet chocolate chips or chunks
¼ cup sliced almonds

Bars
1 cup (2 sticks) unsalted butter, plus more for greasing
1 cup all-purpose flour
1 cup whole wheat pastry flour
1½ teaspoons baking powder
1 teaspoon kosher salt
1½ cups packed light brown sugar
½ cup granulated sugar
2 teaspoons pure vanilla extract
3 large eggs
¾ cup hazelnuts, toasted and chopped

tiny tip: To brown the butter, cook it in a small saucepan over medium heat until it's dark and handsome and smells like the best thing in the world.

1. Brown the 2 sticks butter for the bars (see Tiny Tip) and pour into a glass measuring cup to cool.

2. Meanwhile, make the toffee: Line a quarter sheet (9-by-13-inch) pan with parchment paper.

3. Combine the sugar, butter, and salt in a small saucepan over medium heat and stir slowly with a wooden spoon until a candy thermometer reads 300°F, about 15 minutes. Pour onto the prepared pan, wait 1 minute, then sprinkle with the chocolate. Wait until it melts and spread evenly using a rubber spatula. Sprinkle with the sliced almonds. Place in the freezer for 20 minutes to set.

4. Preheat the oven to 350°F. Grease a 9-by-13-inch pan with butter.

5. To make the bars: Combine the all-purpose flour, whole wheat flour, baking powder, and salt in a large bowl. In the bowl of a stand mixer fitted with the paddle attachment, beat the brown sugar, granulated sugar, vanilla, and eggs on medium speed. Add the cooled brown butter in a steady stream and beat until light and fluffy. Incorporate the dry ingredients 1 cup at a time until mixed.

6. Remove the toffee from the freezer and tap the pan on the countertop to break the candy into jagged pieces. Chop half into bits and stir into the bar batter. Scrape the batter into the prepared brownie pan and smooth the top. Lightly press the remaining toffee into the top of the blondies. Bake for 25 to 30 minutes, until a toothpick inserted into the blondies comes out clean. Cool, slice into 24 rectangles, and pack in a resealable container. The blondies are best eaten within 4 days.

Chocolate Chunk Cowboy Cookies

We've designed this recipe to yield an enormous amount because we love to have extras on hand for spontaneous summer outings. Bake as many as you like; then scoop the extra cookie dough onto a baking sheet using a 2-inch ice cream scoop. Freeze for 1 hour, then transfer the cookies to a gallon-size resealable bag and freeze until ready to bake. When the time comes, bake at 350°F for 17 minutes. No need to thaw in advance. **Makes 42 cookies**

2 cups all-purpose flour
1 teaspoon kosher salt
1 teaspoon baking soda
2 teaspoons ground cinnamon
1 cup (2 sticks) unsalted butter, at room temperature
1¼ cups packed light brown sugar
¾ cup granulated sugar
2 large eggs, at room temperature
2 teaspoons pure vanilla extract
2 cups semisweet chocolate chunks
1 cup unsweetened coconut flakes
1 cup finely chopped pecans
1 cup finely chopped roasted hazelnuts
1 cup rolled oats
Smoked sea salt flakes, for sprinkling

tiny tip: Hit the bulk bins to shop for this recipe without having to rob a bank.

1. Position racks in the upper and lower thirds of the oven. Preheat the oven to 350°F. Line two rimmed baking sheets with parchment paper.

2. Sift the flour, salt, baking soda, and cinnamon into a medium bowl. In the bowl of a stand mixer fitted with the paddle attachment, cream the butter, brown sugar, and granulated sugar on medium speed until pale and fluffy. Add the eggs, one at a time, and the vanilla. Add the flour mixture in three additions, turning the mixer off before each to avoid flour flurries. Stir in the chocolate chunks, coconut flakes, pecans, hazelnuts, and oats.

3. Using a 2-inch ice cream scoop, scoop the cookie dough onto the prepared baking sheets, spacing them 2 inches apart. Sprinkle each cookie with smoked salt. Bake until golden brown, about 15 minutes, rotating the baking sheets once. Transfer the baking sheets to cooling racks and (im)patiently wait for the cookies to reach room temperature. Repeat with the remaining dough. Pack into an airtight container. The cookies are best eaten within 3 days.

Cherry Berry Slump

The slump is a humble confection, both in name and in concept—just add the season's freshest fruit, top with generous dollops of rich, cinnamon-infused cream dumpling dough, and bake. For this version, we use cherries and berries, but if you feel like mixing things up, try strawberries and rhubarb, apples and pears, or a stone fruit medley. **Serves 6**

1 cup whole wheat flour
½ cup plus 2 tablespoons sugar, plus more for the whipped cream
2 teaspoons baking powder
1 teaspoon ground cinnamon
½ teaspoon kosher salt
1 pound pitted cherries, halved
1 pound total blackberries, raspberries, blueberries, and/or strawberries (strawberries hulled and quartered if large)
1 tablespoon fresh lemon juice
1 tablespoon quick-cooking tapioca
1 pint heavy cream

In the Backpack

☐ Large mixing bowls
☐ 10-inch cast-iron Dutch oven
☐ Whisk (see Tiny Tip)

tiny tip: If you forgot the whisk, vigorously shake the cream right in the carton until it's whipped.

At Home

1. Combine the flour, 2 tablespoons of the sugar, the baking powder, cinnamon, and salt in a quart-size resealable plastic bag.

At the Campout

2. Prepare a campfire (see page 24).

3. In a large mixing bowl, combine the cherries, berries, remaining ½ cup sugar, the lemon juice, and the tapioca. In a separate bowl, mix the dry ingredients and 2 tablespoons of the heavy cream, stirring just until well mixed. Divide the dough into 10 pieces.

4. Heat a 10-inch cast-iron Dutch oven over the campfire until hot but not smoking. Pour in the cherry berry filling, then arrange the dough pieces on top, evenly spaced. Put the lid on the Dutch oven and bake at 350°F (7 coals under the oven, 14 on the lid) until the filling is thick and bubbling and the dough is cooked through, 35 to 45 minutes, rotating both the oven and the lid every 15 minutes or so to avoid hot spots.

5. Rinse and dry the bowl you used for the filling and whip the remaining cream in it, adding sugar to taste. Let the slump cool slightly, then spoon it into bowls and top with whipped cream.

Coal-Baked Apples with Cinnamon-Cider Sauce

While divine in the buff, sweet, crunchy Fuji apples reach new heights when stuffed with walnuts, dried fruit, and candied ginger; capped with cinnamon butter; and baked in the campfire coals until tender enough to eat with a spork. Finish them with a sweet-tart cider pan sauce and a splash of heavy cream, and everyone will be licking their enamel bowls clean. **Makes 6**

Cinnamon–Brown Sugar
   Butter (page 130)
½ cup chopped
   toasted walnuts
3 tablespoons
   golden raisins
3 tablespoons dried
   cranberries
1 tablespoon minced
   candied ginger
¼ cup packed dark
   brown sugar
6 Fuji apples
¾ cup apple cider
½ pint heavy cream

In the Backpack

- ☐ Melon baller
- ☐ 10-inch cast-iron
    Dutch oven
- ☐ Barbecue tongs
- ☐ 6 small enamel bowls

At Home

1. Prepare the Cinnamon–Brown Sugar Butter and refrigerate. Combine the walnuts, raisins, cranberries, ginger, and brown sugar in a 1-pint resealable container.

At the Campout

2. Prepare a campfire (see page 24).

3. Use a melon baller to core the apples, stopping about ½ inch from the bottom to create a well. Arrange the apples upright in a 10-inch cast-iron Dutch oven. Divide the walnut mixture evenly among the apples, gently packing it in with the back of a spoon to completely fill the wells. Top with Cinnamon–Brown Sugar Butter, dividing evenly among the apples. Pour the cider into the Dutch oven.

4. Place the lid on the Dutch oven and bake at 350°F (7 coals under the oven, 14 on the lid), until the apples are fork-tender, about 30 minutes, rotating both the oven and the lid halfway through to avoid hot spots. Using tongs, place each baked apple in an enamel bowl. If the cider sauce left in the pan is thin, replace the lid and continue to boil until it is thick and syrupy. Spoon the cider reduction evenly over the baked apples, drizzle each with heavy cream, and serve.

The Great Banana Boat Bake-Off

Cooking competitions are a natural fit for the campground, what with its limited resources, captive audience, and heightened ingenuity, so gather a group for a foil-wrapped showdown.

- Challenge campers to revolutionize the roasted banana by laying out a bonanza of potential toppings, or assigning each camper three to bring. Divine inspiration includes, but is not limited to, chocolate chips, rum, marshmallows, peanut butter, almond butter, sprinkles, salted caramel, bourbon, vanilla, cinnamon, cardamom, caramels, butterscotch chips, banana liqueur, miniature candy bars, pecans, walnuts, coconut flakes, toffee bits, maple syrup, Nutella, jam, flaky salt, and potato chips. Throw in a few red herrings—pickles, sriracha, sardines—to keep the contest interesting.

- Slice the bananas lengthwise, leaving the ends and back peel intact, and tell the competitors to fill the bananas as they please, then inventively wrap them in foil. Bury the bananas in the coals for 10 minutes. Remove, carefully open, distribute tasting spoons, taste, and vote.

- Ten points shall be awarded in each of the following categories:

  Beauty
  Aroma
  Name
  Audacity
  Noshability
  Aftertaste
  Sculpture (of the foil)

- The winner is exempt from dish duty for the rest of the campout.

Molten Chocolate Orange Campfire Cakes

You can have your cake and eat it in an orange, too, with this posh twist on a strange and wonderful camping classic that generally calls for boxed cake mix (hey, we won't judge). Baking time will vary depending on the heat of the coals and how big your oranges are, so check one for doneness before pulling the whole gang off the heat. **Makes 4**

2 tablespoons
   all-purpose flour
½ cup sugar
7 ounces bittersweet
   chocolate, chopped
7 tablespoons
   unsalted butter
4 navel oranges
3 large eggs

In the Backpack

☐ Small saucepan
☐ Melon baller or
   grapefruit spoon
☐ Large mixing bowl
☐ Whisk
☐ Foil
☐ Barbecue tongs
☐ Toothpicks (see Tiny Tip)

---

tiny tip: If you're having trouble keeping the cap atop the orange, secure it with a few toothpicks.

At Home

1. Combine the flour and sugar in a quart-size resealable plastic bag.

At the Campout

2. Prepare a campfire (see page 24).

3. In a small saucepan, melt the chocolate and butter over low heat on the campfire grill grate or over low heat on the camp stove. Set aside to cool. Cut the tops off the oranges, about 1 inch down, reserving the caps. Use a melon baller or grapefruit spoon to hollow out the oranges, reserving the fruit for juice or snacking. Leave the fruit inside the caps intact.

4. In a large mixing bowl, beat the eggs, then slowly add the chocolate-butter mixture in a thin stream, whisking constantly. Add the flour mixture and mix well. Divide the batter among the oranges, replace the caps, double wrap each orange in foil, and nestle them in the hot coals. Bake until the cakes are firm but the centers are still slightly molten, about 30 minutes, turning the oranges halfway through to avoid hot spots.

Double-Decker Pineapple Mug Cakes

Enamelware isn't merely ornamental, it's useful, too, because it's designed to withstand high temperatures. Once you start baking in it, there's just no end to where your serveware-meets-bakeware can go. And so this mug-bound take on the classic, beloved pineapple upside-down cake was born. We like to use rich, syrupy Italian amarena cherries in place of the traditional maraschino, but any cherry on top will do. **Makes 4**

1¼ cups all-purpose flour
1 cup granulated sugar
2 teaspoons baking powder
½ teaspoon kosher salt
½ cup (1 stick) unsalted butter, at room temperature
One 20-ounce can sliced pineapple
2 large eggs
¼ cup plus 1 tablespoon dark rum
4 tablespoons dark brown sugar, plus more for sprinkling
4 cherries

In the Backpack
☐ 4 enamel mugs (see Tiny Tip)
☐ Measuring cup
☐ Mixing bowl
☐ 12-inch cast-iron Dutch oven
☐ Barbecue tongs

At Home
1. Combine the flour, granulated sugar, baking powder, and salt in a quart-size resealable plastic bag.

At the Campout
2. Prepare a campfire (see page 24) and, if using, set up the camp stove.

3. Unwrap the stick of butter (reserve the gooey wrapper) and melt it in an enamel mug over the campfire or on the camp stove. Cool slightly. Use the reserved butter wrapper to grease the inside of three additional enamel mugs.

4. Open the can of pineapple and pour ¼ cup of the juice into a cup. Transfer the flour mixture to a mixing bowl, add the melted butter, eggs, the ¼ cup pineapple juice, and 1 tablespoon of the rum, and mix until smooth. Put 1 tablespoon of the rum and 1 tablespoon of the brown sugar in the bottom of each mug, stir to combine, and add 1 slice of pineapple to each. Distribute the cake batter evenly among the mugs, top with 1 slice of pineapple, sprinkle with dark brown sugar, and put a cherry on top.

5. Place the mugs (see Tiny Tip) inside a 12-inch cast-iron Dutch oven and put the lid on. Bake at 350°F (8 coals under the oven, 14 on the lid) until the cakes are cooked through, 35 to 45 minutes, rotating both the oven and the lid every 15 minutes to avoid hot spots. Remove from the heat, cool slightly, and serve.

tiny tip: Forget your mugs? Just bake the cake the old-fashioned way, directly inside the Dutch oven.

Chapter 6

Fortifications

Being a wilderness warrior (or even just a great outdoors dilettante) works up a mighty thirst, so follow the Scout motto and Be Prepared (to Partake). Whether your taste runs toward no-proof potions like Cucumber-Mint Cooler, individual-flask-portioned Off-the-Grid Old-Fashioneds, or thermos-bound crowd-pleasers like Vanilla Bourbon Hot Apple Cider, this chapter has something for every sipper *and* slurper—the Camp-ari Cup Jelly Shots are on page 177.

5 Furtive Flask Cocktails

When faced with a weekend in the wilderness and/or weight restrictions, pack smart by batching an entire three-to-four-person-tent's worth of cocktails into a classic 8-ounce flask. Mix the booze et al in a spouted measuring cup, swap out traditional garnishes for sweet syrup and citrus oil to avoid inadvertently trapping a berry, and always use a funnel to transfer your own private punch into a flask without losing a drop. Once at the campout, just shake, sip, and pass along (or don't).

Serves 1 to 4, depending on how benevolent you're feeling

---

1. Off-the-Grid Old-Fashioneds

7 ounces rye whiskey
½ ounce maple syrup
½ ounce amarena
 cherry syrup
6 dashes Angostura
 bitters
One 3-inch strip of
 orange zest

Combine the whiskey, maple syrup, cherry syrup, and bitters in a liquid measuring cup. Express the orange peel's oils over the top. Using a funnel, pour into an 8-ounce flask.

---

2. Hideaway Hooch

3 ounces bourbon
1 ounce Clear Creek
 pear brandy
1 ounce St. Elizabeth
 Allspice Dram
3 ounces pear juice

Combine the bourbon, brandy, allspice dram, and pear juice in a liquid measuring cup. Using a funnel, pour into an 8-ounce flask.

3. Badlands Boulevardier

4 ounces bourbon
2 ounces sweet
    vermouth
2 ounces Campari
One 3-inch strip of
    orange zest

Combine the bourbon, sweet vermouth, and Campari in a liquid measuring cup. Express the orange peel's oils over the top. Using a funnel, pour into an 8-ounce flask.

4. Vesper of the Valley

4 ounces gin
2 ounces vodka
2 ounces Lillet Blanc
One 3-inch strip of
    lemon zest

Combine the gin, vodka, and Lillet in a liquid measuring cup. Express the lemon peel's oils over the top. Using a funnel, pour into an 8-ounce flask.

5. Bear Bite

8 ounces Everclear

Using a funnel, pour the Everclear into an 8-ounce flask. At the campout, use to disinfect bothersome wild animal bites.

Thoughts on Thermos Cocktails

When drinking with a pack of parched outdoorspeople who've spent a long day on the trail (be it the Pacific Coast Trail or the paved 100-foot path between the campground and the lake), batching your bevvies is the way to go. And so, the 40-ounce thermos is destined to be one of your most prized camping companions, for both its generous capacity *and* its temperature control capabilities.

Since nothing spoils a party like lukewarm Cucumber-Mint Cooler (page 164), priming your thermos before adding drinks is imperative. For cold drinks, fill your thermos with ice water and let it sit for 5 minutes, then empty and add your cold cocktail, whether it's Blood Orange Bug Juice (page 165) or Big Batch Bloody Mary (opposite).

If your mission is that the Vanilla Bourbon Hot Apple Cider (page 169) live up to its name, fill the thermos with boiling water (not just hot tap water, however tempting it is to take a shortcut), screw on the lid, and let it sit for 5 minutes before pouring it out and adding hot liquid.

This simple step should ensure that your drinks stay satisfyingly hot or cold for up to 12 hours, although we'd be astonished if the Peanut Butter Hot Chocolate (page 168) lasted that long—our personal record is 15 minutes.

Big Batch Bloody Mary

Outfit this beloved brunch beverage for the woods with a healthy pour of pickle juice and a pinecone primp. (Seriously, the pinecone is possibly the best part.) **Serves 6**

3 cups tomato juice
¾ cup pickle juice
  (from a pickle jar)
1 tablespoon
  Worcestershire sauce
2 tablespoons grated fresh
  horseradish
1½ teaspoons sriracha
1½ teaspoons fresh lemon
  juice
¾ teaspoon kosher salt
¼ teaspoon freshly ground
  pepper
6 cornichons
6 olives
6 whole hot chile peppers
6 cherry tomatoes
12 ounces vodka

In the Backpack

☐ Six 1-pint Mason jars

At Home
1. Chill a 40-ounce thermos (see opposite page). Pour in the tomato juice, pickle juice, Worcestershire, horseradish, sriracha, lemon juice, salt, and pepper, seal, and shake to mix.

At the Campout
2. Forage for six thin, strong, 8-inch-long sticks and six pinecones. Sharpen the end of each stick and build each skewer with 1 cornichon, olive, chile pepper, and cherry tomato. Snap a pinecone onto the end of each by wedging the skewer between two petals. Fill six 1-pint Mason jars with ice and distribute Bloody Mary mix evenly among them. Add 2 ounces vodka per jar and mix well. Garnish with the skewers and serve.

Cucumber-Mint Cooler

Nothing beats the summer heat like this crisp cucumber-infused sipper, which is also superb when made with basil, if that's how your garden grows. **Makes 1 quart**

½ cup sugar
2 large cucumbers
  (about 4 cups)
¼ cup fresh mint leaves
Pinch of salt
¾ cup fresh lime juice
  (from about 4 large
  limes), strained
Mint sprigs and lime
  wedges, for garnish
  (optional)

At Home

1. Chill a 40-ounce thermos (see page 162). Bring the sugar and ½ cup water to a boil in a small saucepan. Reduce the heat to maintain a simmer and cook until the sugar has dissolved, 3 to 5 minutes. Remove from the heat and set the simple syrup aside to cool.

2. Cut 8 thin slices from one of the cucumbers and reserve. Peel and coarsely chop the remaining cucumbers, transfer to a high-speed blender, and add the mint leaves, 2 cups water, and the salt. Purée until smooth, 10 to 15 seconds.

3. Strain through a large fine-mesh sieve into a 1-quart measuring cup, stirring and pressing firmly with a spatula to extract as much juice as possible (see Tiny Tip for ideas on what to do with the leftover pulp). Add the lime juice and simple syrup and mix well. Cut the 8 reserved cucumber slices in half (or it'll be a struggle to coax them back out), drop them into the chilled thermos, and add the cooler.

At the Campout

4. Serve over ice, dividing the cucumber slices among the cups, and garnish with mint sprigs and lime wedges, if desired.

---

tiny tip: When you strain the cucumber, save the pulp! Toss it in a smoothie, mix it into muffins, add honey and freeze it into mini pulpsicles, or slather it on as a refreshing all-natural face mask.

Blood Orange Bug Juice

Punch up this summer-camp staple with ripe summer berries, fresh pineapple, and a bright burst of sweet-tart blood orange juice. If you can't find blood oranges, use fresh-squeezed orange or ruby grapefruit juice. **Makes 1 quart**

1 large ripe pineapple, cored and chopped (about 5 cups)
4 cups raspberries (about 2 pints)
1 cup fresh-squeezed blood orange juice
Orange slices or pineapple wedges, for garnish (optional)

At Home

1. Chill a 40-ounce thermos (see page 162). In a high-speed blender, purée the pineapple, raspberries, and 1 cup water until smooth, about 10 seconds. Strain through a large fine-mesh sieve into a 1-quart measuring cup, stirring and pressing firmly with a spatula to extract as much juice as possible. Discard the solids, pour the purée into the thermos, add the blood orange juice, seal, and shake well.

At the Campout

2. Serve over ice, garnished with an orange slice or pineapple wedge, if desired.

Variation

To upgrade to Jungle Juice, mix ¾ cup chilled Blood Orange Bug Juice with 2 ounces vodka and garnish with a wedge of lime.

Starry Sky Masala Chai

Potent green cardamom pods, and lots of them, are the secret to this spicy, aromatic, Mumbai-inspired brew. Seek out the freshest, brightest cardamom pods at your local spice shop or Indian market, and select your ginger carefully, too—using minced dried root versus ground is key. **Makes 1 quart**

50 green cardamom pods
    (about 2 tablespoons)
Two 3-inch cinnamon
    sticks, smashed
1 teaspoon black
    peppercorns
2 bay leaves
1 teaspoon fennel seeds
1½ teaspoons dried minced
    ginger (not ground)
24 whole cloves
    (about 1 teaspoon)
2 teaspoons Assam black
    tea
2 cups milk
¼ cup sugar

At Home

1. Preheat a 40-ounce thermos (see page 162). Pulse the cardamom, cinnamon, peppercorns, and bay leaves in a spice grinder for 10 seconds, or coarsely grind using a mortar and pestle. Mix with the fennel seeds, ginger, cloves, and tea in a small bowl. (Store in a 4-ounce Mason jar if not using immediately.)

2. Combine the milk, chai spices, and 3 cups water in a 3-quart saucepan and bring to a near boil over high heat, then reduce the heat and gently simmer for 10 minutes. Remove from the heat and steep for 15 minutes, stirring occasionally. Using a fine-mesh sieve, strain the chai into a 1-quart measuring cup (it should yield about 4 cups). Discard the solids, rinse the saucepan, return the chai to the saucepan, and reheat on low. Add the sugar and stir until dissolved, then pour the chai into the thermos.

At the Campout

3. Prepare a campfire (see page 24) and fit it with a grill grate.

4. Reheat the chai in an enamel teapot on the campfire grill grate and serve in enamel mugs.

Our Love Affair with Enamelware

Were we to be buried like pharaohs, surrounded by our favorite possessions, you can bet your last marshmallow that archaeologists would discover piles of enamel-encased metal bowls, plates, mugs, teapots, and platters in our tombs. Enamelware is the ultimate camping dishware since it's light, durable, and easily cleaned. What's more, it makes just the right clang when hit by a fork, which is helpful for both summoning (your fellow diners) and shooing away (bobcats). We highly recommend collecting a hodgepodge of new and vintage pieces; chips only add character. The aesthetics—swirled with black-and-white marbling, rimmed with a clean red line, glossed with French blue—are a matter of preference. Personally, we've never seen a piece that didn't make us swoon.

Peanut Butter Hot Chocolate

Also known as the Hibernator, this decadent concoction will give you a head start on your winter coat. For maximum richness, use a high-quality bittersweet chocolate and supersmooth peanut butter. While we're nut butter adventurists in our sandwich-making lives, when it comes to this recipe, you just can't beat Teddie, or good old-fashioned Skippy. **Makes 1 quart**

1½ cups heavy cream
2 cups whole milk
2 teaspoons pure vanilla extract
2 tablespoons unsweetened cocoa powder
2 tablespoons sugar
6 ounces bittersweet chocolate, chopped or chips
½ cup creamy peanut butter
½ teaspoon kosher salt, or to taste
Vanilla Bean Dream Marshmallows (page 140) or Chocolate Marshmallows (page 141), for garnish (optional)

In the Backpack

☐ Medium saucepan
☐ Enamel mugs

At Home

1. Preheat a 40-ounce thermos (see page 162). Combine the cream, milk, and vanilla in a medium saucepan and heat over low heat until warm. Whisk in the cocoa powder and sugar until incorporated, then add the chocolate and whisk until melted. Add the peanut butter and whisk until smooth. Taste and add salt as desired, then pour the hot chocolate into the thermos.

At the Campout

2. Prepare a campfire (see page 24) and fit it with a grill grate, or set up the camp stove. In a medium saucepan on the campfire grill grate or on the camp stove over medium heat, reheat the hot chocolate if necessary. Serve in enamel mugs, garnished with Vanilla Bean Dream or Chocolate Marshmallows (or both), if desired.

Vanilla Bourbon Hot Apple Cider

Because apple cider labeling varies, things can get a bit confusing in the juice aisle; what you're looking for is simply unfiltered, undoctored apple juice, which you're then going to spike with bourbon and spices for a nightcap that will keep people lingering round the campfire playing truth or dare well past bedtime. **Makes 1 quart**

4 cups apple cider
1 tablespoon pure vanilla
  extract
4 cinnamon sticks,
  plus (optional) more for
  garnish
12 whole cloves
1 whole nutmeg
Two 3-inch strips of
  lemon zest
1 cup bourbon

In the Backpack

☐ Medium saucepan
☐ Enamel mugs

At Home

1. Preheat a 40-ounce thermos (see page 162). Combine the apple cider, vanilla, cinnamon sticks, cloves, nutmeg, and lemon zest in a large saucepan. Cover the pan and bring the cider to a simmer, then remove from the heat and let steep for 20 minutes. Strain the cider through a fine-mesh sieve into a 1-quart measuring cup and discard the spices and lemon zest. Pour the cider into the thermos, add the bourbon, seal, and gently shake to mix.

At the Campout

2. Prepare a campfire (see page 24) and fit it with a grill grate, or set up the camp stove. In a medium saucepan on the campfire grill grate or on the camp stove over medium heat, reheat the cider, if necessary. Serve the cider in enamel mugs, with a cinnamon stick garnish, if desired.

Tentside Tea Toddy Bar

The cardigan-with-elbow-patches of cocktails, a hot toddy is classic and comforting in the best way, particularly when sipped bonfireside on a log. The recipe is foolproof; we've never met a toddy we didn't like, and we've met *lots*. If you ask us, every tea is just waiting to be moonstruck by its boozy soul mate. So put the kettle on, set out the honey bear, open your tackle-box tea caddy, unveil a few bottles, and start matchmaking. **Serves 1**

In the Backpack

☐ Tea infuser (optional)

☐ Enamel mugs

Toddy Like So
Combine a tea bag (or loose tea in an infuser), booze, honey, and lemon juice in an 8-ounce enamel mug. Top with hot water and let steep for 3 to 5 minutes, depending on how strong you like your tea. Remove the tea bag or infuser, stir, garnish with a clove-studded lemon slice, and sip the starry night away.

Safari Camp Cuppa

1 bag rooibos tea, or 1 tablespoon loose
   rooibos tea in an infuser
1½ ounces bourbon

1 tablespoon smoked honey
1 teaspoon fresh lemon juice
1 lemon slice, studded with 5 cloves

Base Camp Bergamot

1 bag Earl Grey tea, or 1 tablespoon
   loose Earl Grey tea in an infuser
1½ ounces whiskey

1 tablespoon honey
1 teaspoon fresh lemon juice
1 lemon slice, studded with 5 cloves

Old-Growth Evergreens

1 bag jasmine tea, or 1 tablespoon loose
   jasmine tea in an infuser
1½ ounces St-Germain
   elderflower liqueur

1 tablespoon honey
1 teaspoon fresh lemon juice
1 lemon slice, studded with
   5 cloves

Quiet Hours

1 bag chamomile tea, or 1 tablespoon
   loose chamomile tea in an infuser
1½ ounces apple brandy
1 tablespoon honey

1 teaspoon fresh lemon juice
1 lemon slice, studded with
   5 cloves

Northern Lights

1 pu-erh tea cake
1½ ounces aquavit
1 tablespoon honey

1 teaspoon fresh lemon juice
1 lemon slice, studded with
   5 cloves

MENU

Forest Fiesta

Sup on south-of-the-border
flavors beneath the stars.

Mango Chile Sesame Fruit Rolls 50

Pico de Gallo 201
and tortilla chips

Red Cabbage, Jicama, and Orange Slaw 84

Corn on the Cob with Chili-Lime Butter 70

Catchall Carnitas 106

Double-Decker Pineapple Mug Cakes 156

Let's Talk About Tepache 174

Mezcal-Spiked Camper's Cold Brew 180

Hinterlands Hot Buttered Rum

Otherwise known as the coal-baked apples' tastiest topper, our cinnamon–brown sugar compound butter does double duty in this sweetly spiced haute cocktail. **Serves 4**

½ cup Cinnamon–Brown Sugar Butter (page 130)
¼ cup heavy cream
6 ounces dark spiced rum
1 whole nutmeg (optional)

In the Backpack

☐ Four 8-ounce enamel mugs
☐ Nutmeg grater

At Home

1. Prepare the Cinnamon–Brown Sugar Butter and refrigerate.

At the Campout

2. In each of four 8-ounce enamel mugs, combine 2 tablespoons of the butter, 1 tablespoon of the cream, and 1½ ounces of the rum. Top with hot water and stir to combine. For an over-the-top garnish, grate nutmeg over the top, if desired.

Let's Talk About Tepache

A refreshing, lightly fermented pineapple drink that hails from Mexico, *tepache* is often mixed with beer to up the alcoholic ante (rum, tequila, and mezcal make mixers *magníficos* as well). This version uses the entire pineapple, but you can also make it with just the rinds, in lieu of composting them. This recipe isn't for the instant-gratification seeker; like most naturally bubbly beverages, the secret ingredient is time, so budget two to four days. **Makes 1 quart**

1 small ripe pineapple
1 cup packed dark
   brown sugar
   (see Tiny Tip)
4 whole cloves
1 cinnamon stick
4 to 5 cups filtered water

tiny tip: If you can find *piloncillo*, the traditional Mexican sugar used to make *tepache*, substitute one cone for the brown sugar.

1. Lightly scrub and rinse the pineapple (not so hard that you remove all the natural yeast), trim both ends, and cut it into 1-inch chunks or wedges, leaving the rind intact. You can cut out the core, but it's not necessary. Transfer the pineapple to a half-gallon Mason jar. Add the sugar, cloves, cinnamon stick, and 4 cups water (add more water if necessary to cover), screw on the lid, and mix well. Remove the lid, place a 6-inch square of cheesecloth over the mouth of the jar, and screw the metal band in place, securing the cheesecloth (this deflects any debris).

2. Let the tepache ferment in a warm, dry place (75°F or higher) out of direct sunlight for at least 2 to 3 days. When ready, the tepache will be foamy on top, slightly effervescent, and have a rich, fruity, funky smell. If it turns red or smells off, toss it. If it's not quite ready, ferment it for another day.

3. Skim any white foam on top and throw it away, then strain the tepache through a fine-mesh sieve, reserving the pineapple wedges for snacking and garnish. Refrigerate the strained tepache for up to a week (it will get even fizzier with time). Serve over ice, garnished with a pineapple wedge.

Does a Beer Fit in the Woods?

Why, yes, it does. There's no better way to welcome yourself to camp (after you've pitched the tent and unpacked your cheese-and-charcuterie board) than by cracking open a cold one. Camping and beers belong together. Why else would so many breweries name their beers after natural wonders, after all? (Think Fort Collins Rocky Mountain IPA and Deschutes Mirror Pond Pale Ale.) *My Beer Year* author and certified cicerone Lucy Burningham schools us on how to smartly stock your cooler for a weekend in the woods.

Fresh 'n' Frothy

We live in a golden era when beers in cans aren't just flavorless American lagers. Craft brewers know cans better protect beer from light and oxygen, so you may be getting a fresher beer by buying cans. Plus, they're lightweight, they don't break, and they're easy to recycle—so perfect for outdoor adventures. Or get something fresh on tap and tote it to camp in a growler. These days, many growlers are highly engineered, and some are insulated, which means your beer will stay cold and carbonated for 24 to 48 hours.

Eat Your Beer

Beer can add flavor and texture to everything from pancakes, Middle of Nowhere Mac 'n' Beer Cheese (page 118), and Spicy Chuckwagon Chili (page 108) to beer-can chicken. We're fans of the "Don't cook with anything you wouldn't drink" rule. Choose your brew wisely, though. High bitterness in a beer tends to intensify in a dish, especially one that cooks for a while. For braises, styles like pilsners and stouts work well. Go with a light lager for beer-can chicken. Or brine meats in beer before cooking them. Chicken brined in a citrusy IPA becomes great fodder for the grill.

Strategic Sipping

Think about your beers in three camping courses: daytime drinking (and snacking); dinner pairings; and campfire sipping. When the sun's up, choose beers with lower alcohol content (ABV) and lighter bodies and bitterness, so you're still standing by the time the Sliced Tri-Tip Sandwich Bar (page 94) is ready, and your palate feels fresh—think session IPAs, kölsch, and pilsners. Depending on what's on the menu, dinner could call for a shift to bigger flavors and higher alcohol: saisons, American pale ales, and German lagers. Campfire calls for beers that pair with smoke and sweet-and-sticky s'mores: stouts, porters, a dunkel, or a big, boozy barleywine.

Keep Your Cool

While a dedicated ice-filled cooler is the gold standard of beer-chilling, should a wayward wolverine abscond with your Yeti, you can compensate with all-natural refrigeration methods. Pinpoint the nearest babbling brook; secure your six-pack to a root, stick, or rock; and let the cool water do its work. (Confine loose bottles in a mesh laundry bag or pillowcase first.) If water sources are scarce, dig a hole in a shady patch of soil or sand and bury your beer to its neck to shield it from the fierce summer sun.

Jelly Shots Jubilee

The classier cousins of everyone's favorite spring break party animal, these upgraded jelly shots are made with top-shelf liquor, fresh citrus juices, and homemade simple syrup (see below). **Makes 12**

Simple Syrup

Makes approximately 1 cup

¾ cup sugar
¾ cup filtered water

Bring the sugar and water to a boil in a small saucepan over medium-high heat, then simmer, stirring, until the sugar has dissolved, about 5 minutes. Remove from the heat to cool. Refrigerate in a Mason jar or other airtight container for up to 1 month.

Variation
For Rhubarb Syrup, simmer 1 pound chopped rhubarb in simple syrup for 30 minutes. Strain and reserve the fruit to top flapjacks or ice cream.

Jelly Like So

In a small saucepan, combine the first three ingredients listed in the recipes. Sprinkle the gelatin over the top and let it bloom, about 5 minutes. Heat the mixture over medium-low heat, stirring until all the gelatin has dissolved, 3 to 5 minutes. Add the liqueur, mix well, and distribute evenly among twelve 2-ounce lidded plastic cups. Corral the jelly shots on a rimmed baking sheet, refrigerate for at least 2 hours, garnish (optional), snap on the lids, and stack in the cooler.

Five-Point Buck

1 cup ginger beer
¼ cup fresh lime juice
¼ cup simple syrup
   (recipe opposite)
Two ¼-ounce packets unflavored
   powdered gelatin

½ cup Domaine de Canton
   ginger liqueur
2 tablespoons gin
Pinch of grated lime zest,
   for garnish (optional)

Camp-ari Cup

1 cup ruby red grapefruit juice
2 tablespoons fresh lemon juice
3 tablespoons simple syrup
   (recipe opposite)
Two ¼-ounce packets unflavored
   powdered gelatin

⅔ cup St-Germain elderflower liqueur
3 tablespoons Campari
Candied grapefruit peel,
   for garnish (optional)

Rhubarb and Away

⅔ cup strained strawberry purée
⅓ cup Rhubarb Syrup
   (recipe variation opposite)
2 tablespoons fresh Meyer lemon juice
Two ¼-ounce packets unflavored
   powdered gelatin

⅔ cup rosé
⅓ cup Lillet Blanc
2 tablespoons vodka
Tiny rose petal, for garnish
   (optional)

The Full Moon Monty

Sometimes, sweet boozy jelly shots can lead to au naturel belly flops. If so, here's our eight-step guide to skinny-dipping decorum.

1. During daylight hours, do swimming hole due diligence. During your recon mission, you're looking for proximity to other campers, especially ones with night-vision goggles, stinging nettle patches, large pits concealed with flimsy tree branches, and Sasquatch dens (because you're almost always on the lookout for Sasquatch dens when camping). Remember, an ounce of accidentally-running-bare-bootied-through-a-poison-ivy-patch prevention is worth a pound of Calamine lotion.

2. If you're socializing with proven pranksters, head off post-dip panic at the pass by hiding your clothes after you remove them. (Just don't hide them in a Sasquatch den or poison ivy patch.)

3. More moonlight means greater visibility, so if you're on the "demure" end of the modesty spectrum, wait for cloud cover before casting your cares and corduroys to the wind. Better yet, before you leave home, consult an almanac (or just ask Siri) to find out when the next new moon phase occurs, then schedule your camping trip accordingly.

4. Reluctant disrobers, remember— your body, your choice to float frock-free with the fireflies. If everyone's urging you to join them in the water but you're feeling full-frontal averse, it's perfectly acceptable to wear a swimsuit, your undergarments, or strategically placed fern fronds.

5. It's best to approach the lake, lagoon, or lily pond at a full run, which minimizes both the risk of chickening out and the anguish of that first goose bumps–inducing plunge.

6. If your scenic soak was spontaneous, you'll have to dry off with leaves, bark, or the T-shirt of someone who didn't read tip number 2. If you've pre-planned, have a stack of dry beach towels or ShamWows waiting on dry land.

7. Make only memories, take only memories—no cameras, smartphones, GoPros, or drones allowed. For obvious reasons, particularly if you're a frequently hacked celebrity, dream of a career in politics, or snuck out of the convent to be there.

8. Unless you happen to be roughing it near some hot springs, your pond is probably a bit chilly, so once you've emerged from the water, retrieve your (well-hidden) clothing and hightail it back to camp to set up the Tentside Tea Toddy Bar (page 170). Or build a bonfire on the riverbank and toast your derriere-baring daring with cups of Starry Sky Masala Chai (page 166).

Mezcal-Spiked Camper's Cold Brew

Mezcal's distinctly smoky flavor is cold brew's soul mate; just add a splash of rich coffee liqueur and cinnamon-infused simple syrup, and you're ready to face(plant) the day. This recipe uses perfectly portioned cans of Stumptown cold brew, which we love because they pack and travel effortlessly, but you can always substitute homemade cold brew. **Serves 4**

**Cinnamon Bark
   Simple Syrup**
¾ cup sugar
¾ cup water
2 cinnamon sticks,
   broken into pieces

6 ounces mezcal
2 ounces coffee liqueur,
   preferably House Spirits
Four 8-ounce cans
   Stumptown cold brew
   coffee (see Tiny Tip)
Four 3-inch strips of
   lemon zest

In the Backpack

☐ 4 enamel mugs

At Home

1. To make the Cinnamon Bark Simple Syrup: Bring the sugar and water to a boil in a small saucepan over medium-high heat, then simmer, stirring, until the sugar has dissolved, about 5 minutes. Drop the cinnamon sticks into the pot and simmer for 15 more minutes. Remove from the heat and let steep for 1 hour. Remove the cinnamon sticks and refrigerate the syrup in a Mason jar or other airtight container for up to 1 month. This recipe makes more syrup than you need; use the remainder to sweeten your cowboy coffee or apple cider, pour over waffles, toss with roasted root vegetables, or drizzle over ice cream.

2. Mix the mezcal, coffee liqueur, and 2 ounces of the simple syrup in a stoppered bottle or 1-pint Mason jar.

At the Campout

3. Divide the mezcal mixture evenly among four enamel mugs. Add one 8-ounce can of cold brew to each mug. Add ice cubes, express the oils of 1 strip of lemon zest over each drink, and serve.

tiny tip: For an evening-appropriate twist, switch out the cold brew for hot brew.

A Word on Camp Stove Coffee . . .

Biscuits or pancakes? Bacon or sausage? When it comes to acing a campout breakfast, myriad trails meander to a scenic view and only one plummets off a cliff, and that is: forgetting the coffee. We asked Courier Coffee Roasters' Joel Domreis (aka the coffee expert's coffee expert) to weigh in on how best to brew tentside.

Fresh Prince of Thin Air

Start with the freshest possible beans, roasted in the last two weeks.

Grounds Keeper

Grind your coffee at home and pack it in an airtight container, or bring whole beans and a hand grinder if you have several minutes to walk around the campfire absentmindedly turning a crank. The best on the market, Porlex, hails from Japan and comes in a backpack-friendly miniature format.

Bubble, Bubble, Boil Means Trouble

While Joel generally maintains a laissez-faire attitude toward backwoods baristas ("I mean, it's camping—who cares?"), he won't compromise on water temperature. Coffee is best brewed at 180° to 200°F. To nail it sans equipment, take the (clean, filtered) water off the heat when bubbles just start to form.

Brew Ha-Ha

"My current philosophy is to carry less when I go camping," Joel says. For most, that means brewing with a pour-over cone, an AeroPress, or an unbreakable French press. Joel takes it one step further. He suggests using only a cup, as coffee professionals do when they rate coffee. Here's how to prepare a cupping: Put coarsely pre-ground coffee directly into a mug, pour hot water over it, ignore it for 3 to 5 minutes, then gently push the floating grounds aside with a spoon, a pocketknife, or, for maximum minimalism, your finger, and let them sink to the bottom, leaving you with a rich sipper—and a need for floss, perhaps.

Carry the Remainder

When you're finished imbibing, scoop out the sludge and pack it out.

Chapter 7

Morning Meal

Communing with nature doesn't mean forgoing a civilized brunch, so venture out of the tent, pour a tin cup of Camp Stove Coffee, and let this chapter lead the way to thick wedges of warm Blackberry Cardamom Coffee Cake, bowls of Creamy Cheddar and Bacon Grits, and heaping platefuls of campfire-cooked Smoked Kielbasa, Swiss Chard, and Yukon Gold Potato Hash. Wash everything down with a Big Batch Bloody Mary, and the only thing your mountain air–scented morning meal will be missing is the long wait for a table.

6 Backcountry Breakfast Boards

If you've got a busy day of outdoorsy to-dos ahead and would rather reserve the full English for a more leisurely morning, whip up one of these robust internationally inspired breakfast boards in minutes, using pre-purchased pastries and supermarket staples.

1. **Danish Daybreak**
   Rye bread + seeded bread + Havarti + gravlax + soft-boiled eggs + granola + fresh fruit

2. **Wurst Wake-Up**
   Sausage + salami + ham + cheese + pretzel rolls + jam + butter + soft-boiled eggs

3. **Turkish Daylight**
   Feta + olives + sujuk + hard-boiled eggs + tomatoes + cucumbers + bread + jam + honey

4. **Israeli Daily**
   Baba ganoush + hummus + labneh + cottage cheese + pickled fish + olives + cucumber, tomato, and onion salad + sesame rolls

5. **After Sunrise**
   Croissants + chocolate croissants + pain aux raisins + apricot and strawberry jam + butter + baguette + yogurt + fresh fruit + café au lait

6. **Morning Mahalo**
   Passion fruit + mango + papaya + pineapple + dragon fruit + kiwi + star fruit

The Flaming Paloma

If you love brûléed grapefruit and open flames, this fire-kissed breakfast dish is your spirit animal. Cutting the fruit away from the membrane is optional but makes things easier on eaters, especially if they've already downed a Mezcal-Spiked Camper's Cold Brew (page 180) or two. **Serves 4**

2 ruby red grapefruit
½ cup heavy cream
1 teaspoon granulated
    sugar
1½ teaspoons mezcal
4 tablespoons dark brown
    sugar
Maldon flake salt

In the Backpack

☐ Cutting board
☐ Medium mixing bowl
☐ Propane torch

1. Cut the grapefruit in half and remove any visible seeds. Using a sharp knife, carefully cut around the rim of each half, between the pith and the fruit. Slice between each section to release the fruit from the membrane.

2. In a medium mixing bowl, whip the cream with the granulated sugar, then stir in the mezcal.

3. Pat each grapefruit half dry and sprinkle 1 tablespoon of the dark brown sugar over the top. Using a propane torch or large flaming stick, carefully melt the sugar until golden brown and crisp. Top with a dollop of mezcal whipped cream and a pinch of sea salt flakes, then serve immediately.

Fresh Fig and Summer Berry Jumble

When the fig tree is full and the berry patch is bursting, this blackberry honey–drizzled salad will take a few pints off your plate . . . then put them on your plate. **Serves 6**

1 pint blackberries
1 pint blueberries
1 pint raspberries
1 pint dark cherries, halved
4 large red plums, cut into
   1-inch wedges
4 figs, quartered
¼ cup blackberry honey
1 teaspoon grated lime zest
2 tablespoons fresh lime juice
Fresh mint leaves

On a large platter, artfully scatter the blackberries, blueberries, raspberries, cherries, plums, and figs. Drizzle with the honey, sprinkle with the lime zest and lime juice, garnish with fresh mint, and serve.

In the Backpack

☐ Large platter

Melon, Ginger, and Meyer Lemon Medley

Because there aren't nearly enough opportunities in life to use your melon baller, and because vine-ripened summer melon is as close to the food of the gods as it gets. **Serves 6**

1 honeydew melon
1 cantaloupe
1 seedless yellow
   watermelon
2 tablespoons fresh Meyer
   lemon juice
1 tablespoon minced
   fresh ginger
2 tablespoons crushed
   pistachios
Lemon-thyme sprigs
Maldon flake salt

Using a melon baller, scoop the flesh from each melon and place in a large shallow bowl. Gently toss the melon with the lemon juice and ginger, then sprinkle with the pistachios, thyme, and a pinch of salt to serve.

In the Backpack

☐ Melon baller
☐ Large shallow bowl

Honey-Lime Yogurt Granola Parfaits

To keep these pretty parfaits from suffering a soggy fate, transport the granola, yogurt, and fruit in separate containers, then quickly assemble before serving. If you're a devout do-aheader and want to make them before you leave, that's fine, too, just layer strategically, with the granola on top to help preserve its crispness, then pop them in the cooler. **Makes 6**

Granola (see Tiny Tip)
¼ cup coconut oil
¼ cup maple syrup
1½ cups rolled oats
½ cup coarsely chopped cashews
½ cup coarsely chopped macadamia nuts
½ cup shelled roasted salted pistachios
½ cup hulled raw pepitas
½ cup unsweetened flaked coconut
1 teaspoon kosher salt

Honey-Lime Yogurt
2 cups plain full-fat Greek yogurt
3 tablespoons honey
2 teaspoons grated lime zest

Fruit
1 cup ¼-inch-dice mango (about 1 mango)
1 cup ¼-inch-dice kiwi (about 4 kiwi)
1 teaspoon fresh lime juice
2 teaspoons finely chopped fresh mint

1. Preheat the oven to 300°F. Line a large rimmed baking sheet with parchment paper.

2. To make the granola: In a small saucepan, warm the coconut oil and maple syrup, whisking to combine. In a medium bowl, combine the oats, cashews, macadamia nuts, pistachios, pepitas, coconut, and salt, then add the wet ingredients and stir to combine. Spread the mixture on the baking sheet in an even layer and bake until golden and deeply toasted, 25 to 30 minutes, rotating the pan halfway through. Cool the granola completely before breaking it up, then store it in an airtight container. (This recipe makes double the granola you'll need for parfaits, so pack the leftovers for a quick morning meal, or eat immediately.)

3. To prepare the honey-lime yogurt: In a medium bowl, stir together the yogurt, honey, and lime zest (if assembling the parfaits later, return the mixture to the original yogurt container for transport).

4. To prepare the fruit: In another bowl, mix the mango, kiwi, lime juice, and mint.

5. Divide the yogurt mixture evenly among six tall 8-ounce Mason jars, followed by the fruit mixture and the granola. Screw on the jar lids and refrigerate. Alternatively, pack the ingredients and Mason jars and assemble the parfaits at the campout, layering them so the fruit is on top to better display its comely coloring.

tiny tip: Make the granola ahead of time and store it in the freezer in a Mason jar or other airtight container.

MENU

Two-Skillet Sunrise

Greet the day the best possible way—with boozy cold brew, sizzling skillets, and an abundance of cast-iron-baked carbs.

The Flaming Paloma 186

Fresh Fig and Summer Berry Jumble 187

Egg in a Hole and Bacon on a Stick 192

Smoked Kielbasa, Swiss Chard, and Yukon Gold Potato Hash 202

Buckwheat Buttermilk Flapjacks with Maple Bourbon Butter 204

Dutch Oven Cinnamon Rolls with Orange Almond Icing 214

Blood Orange Bug Juice 165

Mezcal-Spiked Camper's Cold Brew 180

Beet- and Aquavit-Cured Gravlax

Start curing this sunrise-hued salmon two days before you mosey into the mountains, and you'll be rewarded with the prettiest postcard of a brunch spread imaginable. Serve with Horseradish Crème Fraîche (page 95), capers, sliced cucumbers, fresh dill, and thin slices of dense, moist whole-grain rye bread—or bagels, if you're camping in Central Park. **Serves 6**

One 1-pound side of
   salmon, pinbones
   removed
½ pound red beets,
   scrubbed, trimmed,
   and grated
1 teaspoon grated lemon
   zest
½ bunch fresh dill, coarsely
   chopped
1 tablespoon aquavit
¼ cup kosher salt
2 tablespoons sugar
2 teaspoons coarsely
   ground black pepper

1. Pat the salmon dry and lay it skin-side down in a glass baking dish. In a large bowl, combine the beets, lemon zest, dill, and aquavit.

2. In a separate bowl, mix the salt, sugar, and pepper. Spread the cure over the fish, then top with the beet mixture. Cover the salmon with plastic wrap, then place a smaller baking dish on top and weight it down with cans, bottles of Viking Blod, or several copies of the *Noma* cookbook.

3. Refrigerate the salmon for 48 hours, then scrape off and discard the beet mixture. Wrap the salmon and refrigerate for up to 5 days. When ready to eat, remove from the refrigerator and use a very sharp knife to slice the salmon paper thin. Serve immediately.

Egg in a Hole and Bacon on a Stick

Whether you know it as Egg in a Basket, Toad in a Hole, Camper with a Cap, Bro with a Chapeau, Tot with a Tam O' Shanter, Scout with a Stetson, Hen in the Holler, Moon over Miami, One-Eyed Jack, or something else entirely, the storied camping classic of an egg cooked in toast pleases every early riser, particularly those short on patience. (Here's looking at you, kids.) Any bread will suffice, but sweet, eggy challah or a buttery brioche loaf crisps nicely. **Serves 4**

8 slices thick-cut bacon
1 plump loaf of challah, or brioche
1 tablespoon unsalted butter
4 large eggs
Kosher salt and freshly ground pepper
Hot sauce, for serving

In the Backpack

☐ 2-inch biscuit cutter
☐ Rolla Roasters
☐ 12-inch cast-iron skillet

1. Prepare a campfire (see page 24) and fit it with a grill grate, or set up the camp stove.

2. Weave 2 slices of the bacon onto a stainless-steel roasting stick, such as a Rolla Roaster, and rotate over the fire for about 5 minutes until crisp.

3. Meanwhile, ask another camper to slice the bread into four 1-inch slices and use a 2-inch biscuit cutter to cut a hole in the middle of each. (Reserve the cutout middles.)

4. Heat a 12-inch cast-iron skillet on the campfire grill grate or on the camp stove over medium-high heat. Melt the butter in the skillet and place the bread and cutout middles in the pan. Crack an egg into the center of each slice and cook until the bread is toasty and the egg whites are almost set, about 3 minutes. Flip and cook on the other side for 2 minutes. Season with salt and pepper and serve with the cutout middle, the bacon, and a bottle of hot sauce.

Creamy Cheddar and Bacon Grits

Given a little time and a lot of love (in the form of cheese and butter), Low Country's answer to polenta becomes the dreamiest, creamiest bowl of comfort food. This recipe owes its two-cheese trick to the late Bill Neal, of Crook's Corner in Chapel Hill, North Carolina, whose shrimp and grits are the gold standard. **Serves 4**

½ pound bacon,
    finely chopped
1 cup milk
1 teaspoon kosher salt
1 cup stone-ground grits
4 tablespoons (½ stick)
    unsalted butter
¾ cup sharp cheddar
    cheese, grated
½ cup grated Parmesan
    cheese, preferably
    Parmigiano-Reggiano
¼ teaspoon freshly ground
    white pepper
Fresh chives, for garnish

In the Backpack

- ☐ 12-inch cast-iron skillet
- ☐ Medium saucepan
- ☐ Whisk
- ☐ Wooden spoon

1. Prepare a campfire (see page 24) and fit it with a grill grate, or set up the camp stove.

2. Heat a 12-inch cast-iron skillet on the campfire grill grate or on the camp stove over medium-high heat. Cook the bacon until crisp, remove with a slotted spoon, and set aside on a paper towel–lined plate to drain. When cool, crumble the bacon.

3. Meanwhile, bring 3 cups water, the milk, and the salt to a boil in a medium saucepan over medium-high heat on the camp stove. Whisk in the grits and reduce the heat to low. Cook, stirring constantly until the grits are very creamy, about 20 minutes. (If the grits become too thick, stir in a little hot water.)

4. Stir in the butter, cheeses, and white pepper. Taste and adjust the seasoning. Divide the grits among four bowls, sprinkle with the bacon, and garnish with snipped chives.

tiny tip: Leftover grits can be poured into a resealable container, cooled, cut into squares, or into rounds with a biscuit cutter, and panfried in butter.

Mason Jar Lid–Fried Egg Sandwich with Canadian Bacon, Avocado, and Sriracha

Of all the clever camping hacks, and there are so many, we love this one the most. Flip your (Mason jar) lid for a breakfast sandwich that's one part MacGyver and one part McMuffin. The scout leaders at Serious Eats perfected this technique. **Makes 1**

Unsalted butter
1 English muffin
Nonstick cooking spray
1 egg
1 slice Canadian bacon
1 slice Havarti cheese
¼ avocado, thinly sliced
   and fanned out
Sriracha

In the Backpack

- ☐ 12-inch cast-iron skillet
- ☐ Widemouthed Mason jar lids and bands
- ☐ Spatula
- ☐ Butter knife
- ☐ Foil

1. Prepare a campfire (see page 24) and fit it with a grill grate, or set up the camp stove.

2. Heat a 12-inch cast-iron skillet on the campfire grill grate or on the camp stove over medium-high heat. Cut the English muffin in half, butter, and toast, buttered-side down, for 1 minute. Flip and toast for an additional minute. Transfer to a plate.

3. Spray a widemouthed Mason jar lid (both the band and the insert) with nonstick cooking spray and place it in the skillet. Crack the egg into the lid, breaking the yolk for quicker, even cooking. Pour ½ cup water into the skillet to create steam, and cover. Cook for about 2 minutes, until the egg white is set. Using a spatula, remove the egg trap from the heat and flip it over onto a plate, remove the band, and use a butter knife to lift the lid insert off the egg. Place the egg on the English muffin.

4. Pour the water out of the skillet, swiftly cook the Canadian bacon until warmed through, and place on top of the egg. Top with the Havarti, avocado, a drizzle of sriracha, and the other half of the English muffin. Wrap the sandwich in foil and return it to the skillet over low heat until the cheese has melted, about 1 minute on each side. Eat right away, or keep warm over low heat until ready to serve.

Eggs en Cocoa Mugs

Oeufs en cocotte, the classic French breakfast of eggs baked in a splash of cream, goes from café to campfire when enamel mugs stand in for the traditional ramekins. Timing is everything with this dish—you'll know you've nailed it when you're dipping a toast soldier in golden, runny yolk—so err on the side of caution and pull the Dutch oven off the coals early. If extra baking time is needed, replace the hot lid to finish the dish. **Serves 4**

2 tablespoons unsalted butter, plus a bit more to grease the mugs
4 leeks, thinly sliced (see Tiny Tip)
2 garlic cloves, minced
Pinch of kosher salt
4 large eggs
¼ cup heavy cream
1 teaspoon fresh thyme leaves
1 teaspoon minced fresh chives
Country bread, sliced

In the Backpack

☐ Small saucepan
☐ 12-inch cast-iron Dutch oven
☐ 4 enamel mugs
☐ Toaster
☐ Tongs

1. Prepare a campfire (see page 24) and set up the camp stove.

2. In a small saucepan over low heat on the camp stove, melt the butter. Add the leeks, garlic, and salt and stir to coat. Add 2 tablespoons water, cover, and cook, stirring occasionally to make sure the leeks aren't browning, for 15 minutes, until the leeks are tender. (The leek confit can be made at home and packed in, if you prefer.)

3. Heat a 12-inch cast-iron Dutch oven on the coals of the campfire until hot but not smoking, about 10 minutes. Grease four enamel mugs with butter. Divide the leek confit among the mugs and lightly indent the center with the back of a spoon to give the yolk a home. Crack an egg into each mug, pour 1 tablespoon of the cream on top, and sprinkle with ¼ teaspoon each thyme leaves and chives.

4. Remove the Dutch oven lid and carefully pour 2 inches of water into the pot. Place the mugs in the water bath, replace the lid, and bake at 425°F (10 coals below the oven, 18 on the lid) until the eggs are softly set, about 9 minutes. While the eggs are cooking, toast the bread with your Coghlan's Toaster or in a cast-iron skillet, and slice it into soldiers. Remove the Dutch oven from the coals and use tongs to retrieve the mugs. The surface of the eggs should appear jiggly. Let set for 1 minute, then serve with spoons and soldiers.

tiny tip: Save the tough, dark tops of the leeks to make stock.

Spicy Sausage, Roasted Red Pepper, and Smoked Cheddar Breakfast Burritos

While cooking these breakfast burritos the morning of guarantees you the best-smelling campsite on the creek, they also freeze beautifully, so for a make-ahead morning meal *and* improvisational weapon in the case of a Sasquatch attack, assemble them at home, wrap in foil, and freeze. At the campout, tuck them into the coals until cooked through, about 30 minutes. **Makes 4**

Pico de Gallo (page 201)
2 tablespoons Smoked Paprika–Garlic Butter (page 130)
2 red bell peppers
Kosher salt
½ pound russet potatoes (about 1 medium), peeled and cut into ½-inch dice (see Tiny Tip)
1 tablespoon extra-virgin olive oil, plus more if needed
½ pound ground spicy pork sausage
1 small onion, diced
2 garlic cloves, minced
2 teaspoons finely chopped fresh oregano
Freshly ground pepper
8 large eggs
Four 12-inch flour tortillas
4 ounces smoked cheddar cheese, grated
Hot sauce

At Home

1. Prepare the pico de gallo, transfer to a resealable container, and refrigerate. Prepare the Smoked Paprika–Garlic Butter and refrigerate.

At the Campout

2. Prepare a campfire (see page 24) and fit it with a grill grate. Set up the camp stove.

3. Roast the red peppers on the campfire grill grate until charred and soft. Transfer to a paper bag, sweat for 10 minutes, then peel, seed, and slice into ¼-inch-wide strips.

4. On the camp stove, bring a large saucepan of salted water to a boil, add the potatoes, and boil until tender, about 5 minutes. Drain well. Heat a 12-inch cast-iron skillet on the camp stove over medium-high heat or on the campfire grill grate until hot but not smoking, then add the olive oil and brown the sausage. Add the onion and garlic. Cook, stirring, until soft and translucent (add more oil if they're sticking). Stir in the potatoes, oregano, and Smoked Paprika–Garlic Butter and cook until the potatoes are very tender, about 5 minutes. Season with salt and black pepper.

- ☐ Paper bag
- ☐ Large saucepan
- ☐ Colander
- ☐ Two 12-inch cast-iron skillets
- ☐ Foil

5. In a separate skillet, scramble the eggs and season with salt and black pepper. Wrap the stack of tortillas in foil and warm them on the grill grate. Remove the tortillas from the heat, divide the cheddar, eggs, sausage-potato mixture, and red peppers evenly among them, then top each with 2 tablespoons of the pico de gallo and a splash of hot sauce. Tuck in the tortilla sides and roll into a tight burrito. Wrap each burrito in foil and place on the grill grate or in the coals to warm through and melt the cheddar, 5 to 7 minutes, turning occasionally. Serve with additional pico de gallo and hot sauce.

tiny tip: If you have leftover Smoky Smashed Potatoes (page 71), save yourself a step and swap them in for the russets.

Pedal-to-the-Metal Migas

Before you hit the highway, headed for either unknown adventures or straight back into the arms of your beloved Tempur-Pedic and hot water heater, a hearty breakfast is in order. Inspired by versions we've known and loved in Austin, Texas, this scrambled-eggs-meets-crispy-corn-tortillas is a real rib sticker, especially served alongside black beans, fresh avocado, and warm tortillas. Serves 4

12 corn tortillas
8 large eggs
½ teaspoon kosher salt
¼ teaspoon freshly ground
   pepper
One 15-ounce can black
   beans
1 cup vegetable oil
1 tablespoon extra-virgin
   olive oil
1 small yellow onion, diced
1 large poblano pepper,
   diced
1 small jalapeño, finely
   diced
1 large firm ripe tomato,
   diced
4 ounces cotija cheese,
   grated
½ cup chopped fresh
   cilantro
Pico de Gallo (recipe
   follows), for serving
2 ripe avocados, sliced,
   for serving
Sour cream, for serving
Hot sauce, for serving

In the Backpack

☐ Foil
☐ Whisk
☐ Mixing bowl
☐ Small saucepan
☐ 12-inch cast-iron skillet
☐ Slotted spoon
☐ Spatula

1. Prepare a campfire (see page 24) and set up the camp stove.

2. Wrap 8 of the tortillas in foil and place on the fringe of the campfire to gently heat. Whisk together the eggs, salt, and pepper in a mixing bowl and set aside. Pour the black beans into a small saucepan (reserve the can) and warm over low heat. Cut the remaining 4 tortillas into 1-inch strips, then cut the strips into 2-inch rectangles.

3. In a 12-inch cast-iron skillet over high heat on the camp stove, fry the tortilla strips in hot vegetable oil until golden and crispy. Using a slotted spoon, transfer crispy tortillas to a paper towel–lined plate and set aside. (If you'd rather skip the frying, substitute a heaping cup of tortilla chips instead.) Use the black bean can to dispose of the used frying oil.

4. Add the olive oil, onion, poblano, and jalapeño to the skillet and sauté until soft, about 10 minutes. Season with salt and black pepper. Push the vegetables to the side of the pan. Drain off any excess water the tomatoes have released and add them to the skillet, sautéing until some of the water has cooked off, about 2 minutes. Push the tomatoes to the side of the pan and add the eggs. Scramble the eggs, gradually incorporating the sidelined vegetables. When the eggs are nearly finished, mix in the reserved tortilla chips.

5. Remove the skillet from the heat and sprinkle the migas with the cotija and ¼ cup of the cilantro. Serve with warm tortillas, black beans, the remaining cilantro, the pico de gallo, avocados, sour cream, and hot sauce.

Pico de Gallo

Makes about 1 cup

2 medium tomatoes, cut into ¼-inch dice
¼ cup minced red onion
2 garlic cloves, minced
1 small jalapeño, minced (about 1 tablespoon)

¼ cup finely chopped fresh cilantro
2 tablespoons fresh lime juice
Kosher salt and freshly ground pepper

In a mixing bowl, stir together the tomatoes, red onion, garlic, jalapeño, cilantro, and lime juice. Season with salt and pepper. Transfer to an airtight container and refrigerate until ready to serve.

Smoked Kielbasa, Swiss Chard, and Yukon Gold Potato Hash

A quick camp stove parboil ensures that the potatoes fry up evenly, and cooking the hash in stages sidesteps any risk of a mushy mess. Once the hash is finished, crack eggs straight into it, cover, and cook for a one-pan grand slam that will give you plenty of energy to hike, fish, river stomp, and fend off kielbasa-crazed yellow jackets. **Serves 4**

1 tablespoon minced fresh thyme
1 teaspoon kosher salt, plus more as needed
½ teaspoon black pepper
Pinch of cayenne pepper
1½ pounds Yukon Gold potatoes, cut into ½-inch dice
1 bunch Swiss chard, chopped
12 ounces smoked kielbasa, cut into 1-inch rounds, then halved
2 tablespoons extra-virgin olive oil
1 medium yellow onion, chopped
2 garlic cloves, minced
4 large eggs
Hot sauce, for serving (optional)

In the Backpack

☐ 12-inch cast-iron skillet
☐ Large saucepan
☐ Colander
☐ Slotted spoon
☐ Metal mixing bowl
☐ Foil

At Home

1. Mix the thyme, salt, black pepper, and cayenne in a 4-ounce Mason jar. If washing vegetables at the campout isn't your idea of a good time, pre-wash the potatoes and chard.

At the Campout

2. If using, prepare a campfire (see page 24) and fit it with a grill grate. Set up the camp stove.

3. Heat a 12-inch cast-iron skillet on the campfire grill grate or on the camp stove over medium-high heat until hot but not smoking, about 10 minutes. In a large saucepan over high heat on the camp stove, boil the potatoes in assertively salted water until tender but not cooked through, 3 to 5 minutes. Remove from the heat and drain well.

4. Put the kielbasa in the hot skillet and cook, flipping occasionally, until browned and crisp, about 5 minutes. Using a slotted spoon, transfer the kielbasa to a large metal bowl. Add the potatoes and 1 tablespoon of the olive oil to the rendered fat in the pan and cook, stirring occasionally, until golden, 7 to 10 minutes.

5. Transfer the potatoes to the metal bowl, add the remaining 1 tablespoon olive oil to the pan, and cook the onion until soft and beginning to brown, about 5 minutes. Add the chard, garlic, and 2 tablespoons water and cook until the chard is wilted and soft, 5 to 7 minutes. Add the kielbasa, potatoes, and thyme-spice mixture and stir together until well mixed and heated through, about 3 minutes.

6. Make four deep indents in the hash with the back of a spoon and crack an egg into each one. Cover the skillet tightly with a lid, baking sheet, or foil, and cook until the egg whites are cooked through, about 10 minutes. Season to taste and serve with hot sauce.

Buckwheat Buttermilk Flapjacks with Maple Bourbon Butter

Consider this the park ranger of pancake recipes, containing a solution for every camping quandary. We love nutty buckwheat and hearty whole wheat flour for a tentside meal, but any combination of flours, even good ol' all-purpose, works splendidly. For minimal mess, use a gallon-size resealable bag as your batter butler. Simply cut off the corner and pipe away. And while we're prioritizing efficiency, consider melting butter and booze into the syrup *before* the campout with our rich Maple Bourbon Butter topper. Or turn the page for a dozen other ways to spruce up your short stack. **Serves 4**

Pancake Mix
½ cup buckwheat flour
½ cup whole wheat flour
2 tablespoons sugar
1 teaspoon baking powder
½ teaspoon baking soda
½ teaspoon kosher salt

Maple Bourbon Butter
1 cup dark maple syrup
1 teaspoon pure
    vanilla extract
1 cup (2 sticks) cold
    unsalted butter,
    cut into cubes
1 tablespoon bourbon

Pancake Batter
1 large egg
1 cup buttermilk
2 tablespoons canola
    oil, plus more to
    grease the pan

At Home

1. To prep the pancake mix: Combine the buckwheat flour, whole wheat flour, sugar, baking powder, baking soda, and salt in a resealable gallon-size plastic bag.

2. To make the Maple Bourbon Butter: In a medium saucepan, heat the maple syrup and vanilla over medium heat until hot but not boiling. Remove the pan from the heat and whisk 2 cubes of the cold butter into the syrup. Return to low heat and continue whisking in the butter one cube at a time. Do not let the syrup boil, or it will separate. When all the butter has been incorporated, remove the pan from the heat and whisk in the bourbon. Pack in a 1-pint Mason jar and refrigerate. (The syrup will keep for up to 2 months.)

At the Campout

3. Prepare a campfire (see page 24) and fit it with a grill grate. Set up the camp stove.

4. Gently rewarm the Maple Bourbon Butter in a saucepan of water over low heat, keeping the water temperature below boiling.

- ☐ Medium saucepan
- ☐ 12-inch cast-iron skillet
- ☐ Mixing bowl
- ☐ Whisk
- ☐ Wide flexible spatula

5. To make the pancake batter: Heat a 12-inch cast-iron skillet on the camp stove over medium-high heat or on the campfire grill grate. Whisk together the egg, buttermilk, and canola oil in a small mixing bowl. Add the egg mixture to the bag with the pancake mix, seal it, and mush the contents around until just combined.

6. Pour 1 teaspoon canola oil onto a paper towel and swiftly swipe the hot skillet. Using your Swiss Army knife scissors, cut off the corner of the bag and pipe 2 or 3 pancakes, about 3 inches wide, onto the hot skillet. Cook until bubbles form and pop on the surface of the pancake, about 3 minutes. Flip and cook for an additional 2 minutes, until cooked through and toasty. Repeat, brushing the pan with more oil as needed. Stack on a plate, pour on the Maple Bourbon Butter, and eat immediately.

12 Twists on Your Favorite Flapjacks

Butter and maple syrup will always be the original dynamic duo, but to up your top-of-the-flapjack-stack game, try these twelve terrific variations. To prove your topping skills even further, garnish with edible blooms, like pansies, forsythia, violets, wood sorrel, redbud, or chickweed.

1. Grilled pineapple + pineapple syrup + toasted coconut flakes

2. Chocolate chips + Grand Marnier–soaked orange segments + orange zest

3. Cherries + star anise whipped cream + dark chocolate shavings

4. Roasted apples + vanilla bean mascarpone + smoked honey

5. Raspberries + chamomile whipped cream + lemon zest

	6. Blueberries + cardamom whipped cream + toasted pecans
	7. Grapefruit curd + Honey-Lime Yogurt (see page 188) + lime zest
	8. Caramelized bananas + peanut butter sauce + mini chocolate and peanut butter chips
	9. Macerated strawberries + honey mascarpone + basil chiffonade
	10. Pumpkin butter + cinnamon whipped cream + candied walnuts
	11. Brown butter + maple syrup + bacon crumbles
	12. Lingonberry jam + lemon curd + mint leaves

Buttermilk Biscuits

Before they can be flaky and hot, biscuits must be crumbly and *cold*, and there are lots of little tricks to help achieve that, even when baking alfresco. Keep butter and buttermilk nestled in the cooler ice, chill your mixing bowl over ice before using, and run the rimmed baking sheet that serves as your prep station under glacier-cold water before transferring the dough onto it. **Makes 7 biscuits**

2¼ cups all-purpose flour,
    plus more for dusting
2 teaspoons baking powder
½ teaspoon baking soda
1½ teaspoons kosher salt
¾ cup buttermilk
½ cup (1 stick) unsalted
    butter, cut into cubes
Strawberry Rose Icebox
    Jam (recipe follows),
    for serving

In the Backpack

☐ 10-inch cast-iron
    Dutch oven
☐ Rimmed baking sheet
☐ Large mixing bowl
☐ Biscuit cutter or clean
    empty tin can

At Home

1. Combine 2 cups of the flour, the baking powder, baking soda, and salt in a gallon-size resealable plastic bag and refrigerate. Pour the buttermilk into an 8-ounce jar and the remaining ¼ cup flour into a 4-ounce jar and refrigerate.

At the Campout

2. Prepare a campfire (see page 24). Heat a 10-inch cast-iron Dutch oven on the campfire, and dust a rimmed baking sheet with some of the flour from the 4-ounce jar.

3. In a large mixing bowl, combine the dry ingredients and the butter. Rub in the butter with your fingertips (like you're snapping your fingers) until the mixture resembles coarse meal. Add the buttermilk slowly, incorporating it into the dry ingredients with a fork or your fingers, until the dough is fully moistened.

4. Transfer the dough to the baking sheet, gently pat it into a round, and fold it in half. Repeat five times, dusting with flour as necessary, then shape the dough into a 6-by-9-inch rectangle. Dip a 3-inch biscuit cutter

(or clean empty tin can) in the jar of flour and cut out 6 biscuits—press straight down, don't twist, or the biscuits won't rise properly. Use the scraps to form a seventh biscuit.

5. Nestle the biscuits snugly into the Dutch oven and put on the lid. Bake at 425°F (9 coals under the oven, 18 on top) until the biscuits are cooked through and golden brown, about 15 minutes (check at the 10-minute mark to make sure they aren't burning). Serve piping hot, with Strawberry Rose Icebox Jam.

Strawberry Rose Icebox Jam

Unlike its canned counterparts, this soft, spoonable "icebox" jam requires no extra fuss—just gently simmer the fruit, ladle into jars, and refrigerate or freeze. **Makes 12 ounces**

1 pound strawberries, coarsely chopped
¾ cup sugar
1 tablespoon fresh lemon juice
½ teaspoon rose water (see Tiny Tip)

tiny tip: Find rose water at specialty markets or in your neighborhood grocery store's spice aisle.

1. Combine the strawberries, sugar, and lemon juice in a nonreactive bowl and let macerate for at least 30 minutes, stirring occasionally.

2. Transfer the strawberry mixture to a large shallow saucepan and bring to a boil over medium-high heat. Cook until thick and syrupy, 10 to 15 minutes. Remove from the heat and stir in the rose water. If the jam is too chunky for your taste, crush with a potato masher or immersion blender.

3. Ladle the jam into two sterile 8-ounce Mason jars, leaving a ½-inch space between the lid and the top of the jam. Cool to room temperature and refrigerate for up to 2 weeks or freeze for up to 1 year.

Cast-iron Dutch Baby with Grilled Peaches

Aside from a two-year-old traditionalist who, when presented with his Dutch baby, burst into tears and cried, "Dad broke the pancake!," we've never met a camper who didn't delight in this spectacular, oversize popover. To maximize puff and avoid sticking, preheat your Dutch oven until it's piping hot and make sure the eggs and milk are at room temperature. **Makes 1; serves 2**

⅔ cup all-purpose flour
2 tablespoons granulated sugar
⅛ teaspoon kosher salt
4 large eggs
⅔ cup whole milk
4 tablespoons (½ stick) unsalted butter
1 freestone peach
Olive oil
Confectioners' sugar, for dusting
2 lemon wedges
Maple syrup

In the Backpack

☐ 10-inch cast-iron Dutch oven
☐ Whisk
☐ Metal mixing bowl
☐ Grill pan
☐ Cutting board
☐ Mesh sugar shaker

At Home

1. Combine the flour, granulated sugar, and salt in a resealable bag.

At the Campout

2. Prepare a campfire (see page 24) and fit it with a grill grate. If using, set up the camp stove. Heat a 10-inch cast-iron Dutch oven on the campfire.

3. Vigorously whisk the eggs and milk in a metal mixing bowl. Whisk in the flour mixture. Remove the Dutch oven from the fire and add the butter, tilting the oven so that the bottom and sides are coated. Add the batter all at once, cover, and bake at 400°F (8 coals under the oven, 17 on top) until the pancake is golden and puffy, about 25 minutes.

4. Meanwhile, halve the peach and remove the pit. Brush the cut sides with olive oil. On the campfire grill grate or in a grill pan over medium-low heat on the camp stove, grill the peach cut-side down for 3 to 5 minutes, until the peach begins to release its juices. Transfer to a cutting board and slice into wedges.

5. When the Dutch baby is finished, gather an audience for the dramatic unveiling. Move the Dutch baby to a cutting board, slice in half, divide between two plates, and top with peach slices. Sprinkle with confectioners' sugar using a mesh sugar shaker, a fine-mesh strainer, or, in the absence of both, a spoon. Serve with lemon wedges and maple syrup (for those who insist).

Variations

For a **Berry Baby**, top with ½ cup mixed raspberries, blueberries, and marionberries, a squeeze of lemon, and a dusting of confectioners' sugar. For an **Apple Baby**, sauté a thinly sliced apple in the butter for 2 minutes, stir in 2 tablespoons of brown sugar and ¼ teaspoon of cinnamon, then add the batter and bake. For a **Savory Baby**, top with ribbons of thinly sliced ham and Havarti, replace the lid to melt the cheese, and add 2 over-easy eggs.

Blackberry Cardamom Coffee Cake

This marvelously moist morning campfire companion is best served warm straight from the Dutch oven, accompanied by a piping-hot cup of its namesake, obviously. In a perfect campout world, you'd use wild blackberries plucked from a nearby thicket, but in a pinch, farmers' market or frozen will do just fine. **Serves 8**

Streusel
1 cup all-purpose flour
¾ cup hazelnuts, coarsely chopped
¾ cup packed dark brown sugar
1 teaspoon ground cardamom
1 teaspoon ground cinnamon
¼ teaspoon kosher salt
½ cup (1 stick) unsalted butter, cut into cubes

Coffee Cake Mix
2 cups all-purpose flour
1 cup granulated sugar
½ teaspoon kosher salt
½ teaspoon baking soda
2 teaspoons baking powder
2 teaspoons ground cinnamon
1 teaspoon ground cardamom
¼ teaspoon freshly grated nutmeg
1 teaspoon grated lemon zest (from about 1 large lemon)

½ cup (1 stick) unsalted butter, plus more for greasing
2 large eggs
¾ cup buttermilk (see Tiny Tip)
1 cup fresh blackberries

At Home
1. To make the streusel: Mix together the flour, hazelnuts, brown sugar, cardamom, cinnamon, and salt in a large bowl. Using your fingers, work the butter into the mixture until it's coarse and crumbly, then transfer to a 1-quart Mason jar. Refrigerate or freeze the streusel, then pack in the cooler.

2. To make the coffee cake mix: Combine the flour, granulated sugar, salt, baking soda, baking powder, cinnamon, cardamom, nutmeg, and lemon zest in a gallon-size resealable plastic bag.

At the Campout
3. Prepare a campfire (see page 24) and set up the camp stove. Grease a 10-inch cast-iron Dutch oven with butter.

4. Melt the butter in a small saucepan over low heat on the camp stove and let cool. Whisk together the eggs, buttermilk, and melted butter in a small mixing bowl. Transfer the cake mix to a large mixing bowl, add the wet ingredients, and whisk until smooth. Pour half the batter into the Dutch oven and top with half the streusel, then repeat with the remaining batter and streusel. Sprinkle the blackberries evenly over the top, pressing them lightly into the streusel.

In the Backpack

- ☐ 10-inch cast-iron Dutch oven
- ☐ Small saucepan
- ☐ Small mixing bowl
- ☐ Whisk
- ☐ Large mixing bowl
- ☐ Spatula

5. Put the lid on the Dutch oven and bake at 350°F (7 coals under the oven, 14 on the lid), rotating both the oven and the lid every 15 minutes to avoid hot spots, until the coffee cake is baked through, 50 to 60 minutes. Remove the oven from the coals and let it rest for 15 minutes with the lid on, then cut the cake into wedges and serve warm.

tiny tip: Left your Pyrex back in civilization? Use a Mason jar to measure the buttermilk.

Dutch Oven Cinnamon Rolls with Orange Almond Icing

Fortified with fragrant orange zest and *plenty* of butter, these ooey-gooey cinnamon rolls will lure even the most reluctant riser out of the tent. Make them at home as far ahead of time as you wish—after slicing the dough into rounds, nestle them into a resealable plastic container and refrigerate or freeze. Thaw at the campout and bake, or, in a pinch, lash them together to build a makeshift raft. **Makes 12**

Dough
1 cup whole milk
6 tablespoons (¾ stick) unsalted butter
4 cups all-purpose flour
One ¼-ounce packet active dry yeast (about 2¼ teaspoons)
¼ cup granulated sugar
1 teaspoon kosher salt
2 large eggs, at room temperature

Icing
4 ounces cream cheese, at room temperature
2 tablespoons unsalted butter, at room temperature
⅓ cup confectioners' sugar
2 tablespoons sour cream
1 teaspoon grated orange zest (from about 1 small orange)
⅛ teaspoon pure almond extract

At Home
1. To make the dough: Stir together the milk and butter in a small saucepan over low heat until melted and very warm to the touch, 120° to 130°F, then remove from the heat. In the bowl of a stand mixer, combine the flour, yeast, granulated sugar, and salt. Using the dough hook, mix the ingredients on low until combined, 10 to 15 seconds. With the mixer running, add the eggs one at a time, then add the milk-butter mixture in a slow stream. Knead on the lowest speed until the dough is smooth, shiny, and elastic, about 10 minutes. Transfer to a large greased bowl, cover with a kitchen towel, and let rest in a warm spot for 60 to 90 minutes, until doubled in size.

2. To make the icing: While the dough is proofing, beat the cream cheese and butter with a hand mixer until smooth, then add the confectioners' sugar and beat until creamy. Mix in the sour cream, orange zest, and almond extract until smooth. Transfer the icing to a widemouthed 8-ounce Mason jar and refrigerate or freeze.

3. To make the filling: Combine the brown sugar, cinnamon, and orange zest in a medium bowl, using your fingers or a spatula to crush any lumps, until the mixture resembles wet sand. When the dough has nearly finished proofing, melt the stick of butter in a small saucepan and remove from the heat to let cool slightly. Punch

Filling

1 cup packed light
  brown sugar
2 tablespoons ground
  cinnamon
2 teaspoons grated
  orange zest (from
  about 1 large orange)
½ cup (1 stick) unsalted
  butter

1 tablespoon unsalted
  butter, for greasing
Grated orange zest
  (optional), for garnish

In the Backpack

☐ 12-inch cast-iron
   Dutch oven

down the dough, then roll it into a 12-by-18-inch rectangle. With a pastry brush, spread the melted butter over the dough, then sprinkle the filling evenly on top. Roll the dough lengthwise into a tight log and crimp the edge tightly to seal. Use a tape measure and paring knife to mark 1½-inch rounds, then slide a piece of dental floss or fishing twine underneath, cross the ends, and pull firmly, cleanly slicing each roll. At this point, the rolls can be placed in a resealable plastic container with parchment paper between the layers and refrigerated or frozen.

At the Campout

4. Prepare a campfire (see page 24). Grease a 12-inch cast-iron Dutch oven with the butter.

5. Unwrap and arrange the cinnamon rolls in a single layer in the oven. Put on the lid and let the rolls rest in a warm spot near the fire (rotating occasionally to avoid overheating) until puffy and nearly doubled in size, about 1 hour.

6. Bake the rolls in the Dutch oven at 350°F (8 coals under the oven, 14 on the lid) until the they are cooked through, 15 to 20 minutes. Remove the oven from the coals and let the rolls cool slightly. Spread the icing on top (for extra orange oomph, sprinkle additional zest on top) and serve immediately.

Until We Camp Again

Summer, in all its fleeting, gorgeous glory, contains the better part of our favorite memories. The weather sets it apart, of course, but we think it's that shift in the axis of our priorities, allowing more hours for friends and fun and less for worry and work, that makes an impression. It doesn't take much effort to make summer delicious; one only needs to make time for it. That goes for the food, too.

It's hardly a coincidence that we're all happiest in the summer, when we spend the most time outside. More than anything, we hope that you'll see camping as a reason to explore the beautiful places around your home, and that you'll be a trustworthy camper when you do. While we're advocates of making outdoor living as

comfortable as possible, we're also rather persnickety about leaving the campsite better than we found it, packing out everything we bring in (including recyclables when bins are not provided), and, once home, supporting the conservation efforts of the nonprofit organizations we admire. On a small scale, we think the best thing you can do for the environment is to bring your friends outside. In our experience, most avowed noncampers can be swayed when they realize that camping actually amounts to a fantastic sleepover party.

A campout is a return to straight-up wonder, a chance to celebrate the elemental pleasures of our wonderful world: food, laughter, nature, music, fellowship, and adventure. It's an opportunity to succeed imperfectly, to recognize that the charred bits made the dish better and that there's usually another marshmallow if you drop one in the fire. It's permission to live loosely, eat a series of meals topped with melted cheese, wear the same sweater for days or swim in your skivvies, zip together sleeping bags, feign expertise, whisper in the dark. We wish you marvelous excursions, outrageous campfire stories, and the ability to spot the perfect roasting stick from a mile away. We hope you'll be a happy camper, always.

Camp Provisions

Fantastic Food and Drink

Bella Viva Orchards
bellaviva.com
Whatever organic dried fruit strikes your gorp-making fancy, this California orchard has it.

Clear Creek Distillery
clearcreekdistillery.com
Fine Pacific Northwest fruit-based spirits, including a signature pear brandy, Douglas fir brandy, and marionberry liqueur.

Freddy Guys
freddyguys.com
Prepare to be spoiled for any other hazelnut after you've tried these Willamette Valley–grown wonders.

Marshall's Haute Sauce
marshallshautesauce.com
The camp kitchen simply isn't complete without a set of these hotsy-totsy and tasty sauces and spice rubs.

Olympia Provisions
olympiaprovisions.com
Old-world-style cured meats, sausage, pâté, rillettes, and pickles.

Rancho Gordo
ranchogordo.com
Game-changing heirloom beans.

Underberg
underberg.com
Diminutive digestifs designed to soothe stressed stomachs. Signature twenty-bottle belt highly recommended.

Sporks, Skillets, and More

Anthropologie
anthropologie.com
All the outdoor accessories necessary to glam up a campout, from metalwork lanterns to macramé hammocks.

Big Agnes
bigagnes.com
Couples' sleeping bags with built-in mattress pockets, so you'll never fall off a pad again.

Coleman
coleman.com
Outdoor equipment specialists extraordinaire—from tents and screen shelters to coolers, stoves, lanterns, enamelware, egg carriers, and waterproof playing cards.

Danner
danner.com
American-made hiking boots that are equally stylish and sound.

Filson
filson.com
Sturdy, elegant outdoor clothing and accessories for you and your pup, and highly covetable Chelan camp chairs.

Finex
finexusa.com
The stone-cold stunners of cast-iron cookware proudly made in Portland, Oregon.

IKEA
ikea.com
From two-dollar utensil sets to ten-dollar chef's knives, inexpensively accessorize your camp kitchen in the cooking department.

JK Adams
jkadams.com
Stunning Vermont-made wood cutting and carving boards, backed with a lifetime guarantee.

Le Creuset
lecreuset.com
Neither snow nor rain nor heat nor gloom of night stays these revered Dutch ovens, skillets, and griddle pans.

L.L. Bean
llbean.com
Camp stoves, camp furniture, folding camp kitchens, fire pits, enamelware, and other gear galore.

Lodge
lodgemfg.com
Iconic American-made cast-iron skillets, Dutch ovens, griddles, lid lifters, camp tripods, and outdoor kitchen accessories.

Nikwax
nikwax-usa.com
Products to waterproof just about anything, and wash all the outdoor gear you heretofore considered impossible to clean, including down sleeping bags.

The North Face
thenorthface.com
Iconic high-performance activewear and gear for both extreme and not-so-extreme outdoorspeople; the nearly indestructible laminate duffel bags make the best possible camping supply carriers.

The Okee Dokee Brothers
okeedokee.org
Not-crazy-making children's music from a duo whose outdoor adventures inspire road trip–ready albums. Start with *Can You Canoe?*

Pendleton
pendleton-usa.com
Beautiful and timeless patterned wool blankets made in the Pacific Northwest.

Poler
polerstuff.com
Innovative camping gear that inspires coinage, including the square skillet (*squillet*), the wearable sleeping bag (*napsack*), and the car-top-mounted *le tente*.

REI
rei.com
The name—Recreational Equipment, Inc.—says it all, and they've got it all, from wood-burning camp stoves and collapsible cook stations to every kind of cooler under the sun. Plus, it's a co-op. Members receive 10 percent back on all purchases as a dividend of the annual profits.

Rolla Roaster
rollaroaster.com
The original rotating marshmallow roasting fork.

Rome
romeindustries.com
Round, square, heart-shaped, double wide—whatever type of cast-iron pudgie pie iron you seek, they've got it.

Rove and Swig
roveandswig.com
Enamelware *everything*.

Snow Peak
snowpeak.com
Aesthetes adore this Japanese-designed outdoor line.

Stanley
stanley-pmi.com
Heavy-duty vacuum bottles and crocks, flasks, beer growlers, travel mugs, and coolers.

Staub
staubusa.com
Handsome fire-friendly French-made cast-iron Dutch ovens, grill pans, braisers, skillets, and kettles.

Target
target.com
Camp kitchen accessories, cheap 'n' cheerful dishware, barbecue tools, portable picnic tables, and collapsible wagons to schlep it all.

Thermacell
thermacell.com
Scare away skeeters with a device that delivers a 15-by-15-foot bug-free zone.

Thermoworks
thermoworks.com
Super-cute, super-quick, and super-accurate meat thermometers.

Yeti
yeti.com
An ice chest for every appetite.

Acknowledgments

We award the Best Editor and All-Around Delightful merit badge to our amazing editor, Judy Pray, who makes this whole process a walk in the woods. We're forever grateful for her invaluable guidance and sage city-girl insights. And to Emily Isabella, Michelle Ishay-Cohen, and Renata Di Biase, the Wit, Wiles, and Watercolors badge for bringing our dreams to life, yet again. We'd be up a creek without you.

To Sharon Bowers and Stacey Glick, the Ace Agenting badge. To Lia Ronnen, the Cleverest Publisher badge. We're honored to be Artisan authors, and we cheerfully award badges to the extraordinary troop: Bella Lemos (Mastery in Juggling and Trail Mix Production), Ivy McFadden and Sibylle Kazeroid (Best Pesto Oxidation Preventer and Thwarter of Danglers), Nancy Murray and Hanh Le (Devotion to Details, Details), Zach Greenwald (Excellence in Punctuality and Patience), and Theresa Collier and Allison McGeehon (Superlative Horn Tooting).

We award the Relatively Stoic in the Face of Severe Test Kitchen Chaos and Always Up for a Last-Minute Sur La Table Run badge to Jeff, and to Jamie, the Loyal Keeper of the Backyard Fire Pit and Finest Flask Cocktail Tester badge. For James, the Most Honest Feedback badge, and to Cal, the Most Darling Distraction badge.

To Jen's parents, who insisted that roughing it under the stars was better than any five-star hotel, the Thanks a Heap . . . No, Really! badge. And to Marnie's parents, who insisted that she try everything once regardless of natural affinity, the Participation Against the Odds badge, with an additional bonus Shake the Tent with Laughter badge to her sister, Maggie, and her cabinmates at Kamaji.

And finally, the Most Enthusiastic Tongue Scrubbing of an Unattended Dutch Oven Roast Chicken merit badge goes to our furry camp kitchen mascot, Winnie, who is with us every step of the way—mostly because she's sure we'll turn our back on the provisions at any moment, but still.

Index

Conversion Charts

Here are rounded-off equivalents between the metric system and the traditional systems that are used in the United States to measure weight and volume.

FRACTIONS	DECIMALS
⅛	.125
¼	.25
⅓	.33
⅜	.375
½	.5
⅝	.625
⅔	.67
¾	.75
⅞	.875

WEIGHTS

US/UK	METRIC
¼ oz	7 g
½ oz	15 g
1 oz	30 g
2 oz	55 g
3 oz	85 g
4 oz	110 g
5 oz	140 g
6 oz	170 g
7 oz	200 g
8 oz (½ lb)	225 g
9 oz	250 g
10 oz	280 g
11 oz	310 g
12 oz	340 g
13 oz	370 g
14 oz	400 g
15 oz	425 g
16 oz (1 lb)	455 g

VOLUME

AMERICAN	IMPERIAL	METRIC
¼ tsp		1.25 ml
½ tsp		2.5 ml
1 tsp		5 ml
½ Tbsp (1½ tsp)		7.5 ml
1 Tbsp (3 tsp)		15 ml
¼ cup (4 Tbsp)	2 fl oz	60 ml
⅓ cup (5 Tbsp)	2½ fl oz	75 ml
½ cup (8 Tbsp)	4 fl oz	125 ml
⅔ cup (10 Tbsp)	5 fl oz	150 ml
¾ cup (12 Tbsp)	6 fl oz	175 ml
1 cup (16 Tbsp)	8 fl oz	250 ml
1¼ cups	10 fl oz	300 ml
1½ cups	12 fl oz	350 ml
2 cups (1 pint)	16 fl oz	500 ml
2½ cups	20 fl oz (1 pint)	625 ml
5 cups	40 fl oz (1 qt)	1.25 l

OVEN TEMPERATURES

	°F	°C	GAS MARK
very cool	250–275	130–140	½–1
cool	300	148	2
warm	325	163	3
moderate	350	177	4
moderately hot	375–400	190–204	5–6
hot	425	218	7
very hot	450–475	232–245	8–9